T0196603

SUPRIYA

The Nun Who Went to Prison

Supriya Deas

BALBOA
PRESS

A DIVISION OF HAY HOUSE

Balboa Press books may be ordered through booksellers or by contacting:

Balboa Press
A Division of Hay House
1663 Liberty Drive
Bloomington, IN 47403
www.balboapress.com
1 (877) 407-4847

Illustrations by Isaac Deas, copyright © 2014.

Print information available on the last page.

ISBN: 978-1-5043-2746-6 (sc)
ISBN: 978-1-5043-2748-0 (hc)
ISBN: 978-1-5043-2747-3 (e)

Library of Congress Control Number: 2015901596

Balboa Press rev. date: 2/24/2015

I DEDICATE THIS BOOK TO all victims of crime. From the bottom of my heart, I offer sympathy, compassion, and encouragement on your journey to peace.

And I dedicate it to the vast array of men, women, and children who visit loved ones in prison. I know firsthand the crowded waiting rooms, invasive searches, fear for the prisoners' safety, and disappointment that arises when they reoffend right before their parole date.

I also dedicate this book to all offenders who are locked in cages, immersed in violence, and expected to come out as respectable, law abiding members of society. May all your bitterness, shame, and anger be spiritually released and any harm done or received be forgiven.

And to the prison guards, grocery clerks, and landlords who take a step back when they hear of our plight—like us, they too need a little forgiveness sometimes.

And last but not least, I dedicate this book to my spiritual master Baba Hari Dassji and my beloved son, Isaac Deas. It is through your extreme life examples that you proved that the ancient teachings of peace really do set us free.

CONTENTS

FOREWORD
by Isaac Deas

FIFTEEN YEARS AGO, I FOUND myself in a deep, dark hole. I was feeling miserable as I had lost my way in life. I had given up hope that anyone cared about me and was afraid of what my future held. Days turned into months and months turned into years, and then one day, I heard a voice calling, "Hello? Is anyone down there?" It was the sweetest voice I had ever heard.

"Hello? Can you help me?" I answered, and an angel descended into my dark hole, bringing with her the help I needed to get out of the prison I was in.

That angel never left. She stayed by my side and continued to help me along the way, ever guiding with a gentle hand and wise word. As I grew stronger and began to heal, she said, "The secrets are here in this book which I give to you. Many will read it and come to know the strength of faith and love. These are my secret dreams."

That angel, all dressed in white, is my mother, Supriya, whom I love with all my heart. When everyone else gave up on me, she never did. This book will touch you like no other. Her secret dreams remind us that if we will follow our dharma, all will be revealed.

PREFACE

I N 1997, I FOUND MYSELF divorced; the mother of three troubled adult children; and in excruciating mental, emotional, and spiritual pain. It had been five years since my son Isaac had gone to prison, and he was getting worse, not better. Desperately seeking peace, I decided to go to an ashram in California to study with my yoga master, a silent monk from India.

Eager to attain even a semblance of his inner radiance, I went to every class, learned all the mantras, and practiced the breathing and meditation techniques every day. I flourished in the working spiritual community, and during my second year, I took vows as a yogic nun so I could dedicate the rest of my life to serving God.

Isaac and I kept in touch through letters, phone conversations, and yearly "trailer visits," which are private family visits of up to 72 hours' duration in a walled off section within the prison grounds. Each time he was about to go up for parole, something happened to set him back that, of course, was never his fault.

And then one morning, my inner voice told me it was time to go to the prison and help my son. When I announced my decision to family and friends, they assured me that it was a mistake; my mission would be futile.

"Stay where you are. You're happy and safe at Mount Madonna."

"You can't even speak French."

"Where will you live?"

"You will fall spiritually if you leave the ashram!"

"You don't have money or a job. How will you live?"

"Criminals are dangerous!"

"People who have gone to prison can't be helped."

When I told my guru that I was going, his answer was simple: "It is your duty," he wrote on his chalkboard.

Once I got to Quebec, I often kept to myself, especially in the evening. As I moved from place to place, my boarding rooms or small apartments were quickly transformed into temples decorated with candles, flowers, and pictures of my guru and other saints. Worship and meditation replaced television, and my determination to get my youngest son out of prison kept me focused and full of energy.

It is now 2015, and I am editing my book for publishing. Although composed as a parable, most of the experiences and conversations in this book are real. I smile as I read back over our courageous journey, for now I know for certain that dreams really do come true. And now, I invite you to keep an open mind and enjoy my tale of unconditional love.

ACKNOWLEDGMENTS

I SINCERELY THANK MY CHILDREN Joshua and Terra for their understanding and support during the years I spent helping their brother in prison; my dear parents, John and Mary, who taught me non-attachment and undying love; and my brothers, Don and Bob, who offered money, shelter, and encouragement when I needed it the most.

Special thanks to Christine Brown for her friendship and helpful contacts; Greta Chandrika Tabachnick, who surprised me with transportation and shelter from clear across the country; Sylvain Robillard, Louise Carle, France and Jean Deslauriers, Don and Jacqueline Craig, Brigitte Lemay, Francine Desjardines, Joanne Francouer, Sylvie Poisson, and Josée and Eric Méthot, who graciously welcomed me, a complete stranger, into their homes.

Thanks so much to my good friends, Ben Nickerson, for generously paying all the three-way phone calls during prison transfers; Cynthia Moore for rekindling our teenage camaraderie; and Christine Hinch and Sam Maniatis of Total Home Training for financially sponsoring my first book.

My immense gratitude to Jodi and Dona Cadman for this incredible journey of forgiveness; my deepest respect and appreciation to Baba Hari Dassji, who taught me to love without condition; and untold blessings to my son Isaac, for allowing me to walk beside him during the last ten years of his incarceration and beyond his final release.

CHAPTER 1

The First Day of the Rest of Your Life

THERE WAS ONCE A WOMAN who very much loved to bring peace to the downtrodden people of her village. She knew that if they would just follow the path of righteousness, all suffering would cease. People are weak, she knew from her own experience, and there is a slow, steady climb that everyone must take. The quickest way to get to the place of peace is through gratitude, faith, and prayer.

One day she had an idea that sparked the interest of several people. She took photographs when no one was looking. These photographs were not your average black-and-white or colored film, but they were inside the woman. She carefully observed what made people tick. When she saw the fire inside of them that brought forth their very best, she took a picture. No one but her could see these photographs because they were inside her own mind.

But one day they will see! One day I will help them realize their own true natures, and all suffering will cease.

She got out her tablet.

"Today is the first day of the rest of your life," she began, and then she listed all of the people's names she wanted on her team.

She thought, *What the heck? I can always ask!*

Next, she began to draw. These drawings were not ordinary drawings but ones divinely brought forth from within. She put the paper in front of her and had markers close at hand. By the time she was finished, she had several pages with the directions needed to begin the life she had always been preparing for.

Her God was love, and she knew that if she just loved people, they would begin to love others. If she cooked for them, they would learn how to eat well, and one day, they too would pass that along to someone else. If there was enough support for people to bring forth their true hopes and dreams, they would not need to make other people miserable by robbing them of theirs, and selfishness would fade into universal love.

The one thing the woman didn't know was that several other people were praying for the same thing. The only difference was that they did not have the fortitude to step forward and make their dreams come true. When she realized the energy she was capable of sharing with others, she began to pray the way St. Francis of Assisi had long before her.

"Dear Master," she asked with great humility and sincere devotion. "Won't you let me be an instrument of your peace? I'm willing to do whatever it takes, my Lord, to bring love where there is hatred, forgiveness where there is injury, faith where there is doubt, truth where there is error, joy where there is sadness, and where shadows lurk, let me bring light!"

The years had proven to her that self-seeking comforts only brought pain and that the desire to be understood and loved brought nothing but misery. She asked God to please let her seek to comfort rather than to be comforted, to understand rather than wanting to be understood, and to love instead of trying to get love for herself. As she prayed, she began to know that by giving, one receives and that by pardoning, one is pardoned. Through these realizations, she became aware that when the selfish parts die, only then does one awaken to eternal light. And so it came to be.

Chapter 2

A New Day Is Coming

Now one day, the woman had the desire for her husband of days gone by to come to work with her and for their family to have the chance to become one as they once were. She'd always believed in the family unit but did not have the basic principles needed to make it harmonious.

Her youngest son was her ally, she thought, but he was actually tearing her dreams apart, bit by bit. He spoke about losers like he had a bad taste in his mouth and wondered why his mother couldn't see things his way. He'd begun doing religious rituals with her and drawing pictures of saints by making tiny circles with his pens. He even did the spiritual austerities of his mother, but it was all just a lure to keep her nearby.

She didn't try to teach him anymore because he was once again in control and he wanted to keep it that way. Her eldest son began making his way in life, encouraging his younger brother through letters and phone calls. His mother was pleased to see their attachment, thinking that it was the basis of a family unit.

Attachment will hold us together, she told herself. *Blood is thicker than water. Look at my brothers. They do everything for their kids!*

She suddenly remembered the words of her spiritual master.

"Ego, attachment, and desire," he'd written. "These are the three-headed demon that must be slain. With attachment comes pain, because all attachments eventually break when someone leaves home, divorces, or dies. The ego actually thinks it's the boss and will never desert the spirit. But the truth is, God is the all in all, the one in many and many in one. Ego is only a function, an evolute of the mind."

As the woman pondered these things, she thought, *What about desire? Must all desire go too?*

"No," her teacher explained, again and again. "The desires must be turned toward spiritual evolution. We can't start at the top of the ladder and expect to be where others are without taking the same steps they took."

The woman went back to her writing. She knew that the root of her spirituality had something to do with her writing but didn't know how to teach her son about faith without getting ridiculed. The face of the prison chaplain popped into her mind.

"I saw you on my way to the prison today," he admitted. "I was going to stop and offer you a ride, but I was afraid you would get angry or reject my kindness. You were walking with such great determination. It was snowing, and you looked so cold. I almost turned around and went back for you."

The woman gave him some very appropriate advice. "Even if people reject you, you must still offer to help them. If they refuse your kindness 108 times, you must offer the 109th time and they might take the glass of water. When the glass of water is finally accepted, you have done your duty. The duty was not to get them to drink but to build your own strength of character. If you offer what is in your heart, you are living the truth. That is when the principle of *truth* will live through you and *peace* will reign supreme."

The priest liked the woman's advice, but her son was a little dismayed. He liked to compare himself to others, so when he saw his mother light up while talking to the priest, he became a little distracted.

Why isn't my mother's attention on me? This visit is all about me, and she is neglecting to speak of me, introduce me, or like me in any way because she prefers the priestly type much better than the con.

It was then that he saw the error of his ways. He suddenly remembered something his mother had told him when she was just beginning her own spiritual journey.

"I burned all my old photographs that made me feel bad. I was fed up with trying to live up to other people's ideals. I was never enough! My father wanted me to dress in stylish clothes and wear my hair a certain way. When I was in high school, my eldest brother wanted me to be a cheerleader, but I was a scholar, a nerd. All I wanted was to study and dig deep into the archives at the library.

"'What's wrong with me?' was my mantra and 'How does God want you to be?' the guru's advice. That was when I realized the guru could not direct me in a worldly fashion because the guru is spiritual!"

Throughout the woman's life, these deep, searching thoughts plagued her. As she grew older, she began to see how the world reflects the inner workings of the mind, but she did not understand the common bond between the two.

"The world is a mirror in which God's image reflects," her teacher, the silent monk, had written on his chalkboard many times, trying to help his devotees understand the true nature of worldly existence.

"Go to the spiritual root," great sages advised once they had completed their spiritual journeys.

One night after leaving the prison, the woman stayed in a bed and breakfast. Literally everything—the lamps, the chairs, and even the end tables—had a price tag. She felt like she was living in a gift store.

That's it! she thought. *I'll pay my ex-husband back for all the work he did in my gift store after I'd already left him to find the Truth. He won't understand, but that doesn't matter. I will practice the principles that St. Francis taught: seek to understand, not to be understood.*

It was then that she finally understood what she had been doing wrong. She was trying to understand people instead of God.

The world is a mirror in which God's image reflects!

Her mission was becoming clearer and clearer.

The woman prayed, *What about my son? He doesn't seem very happy about his father.*

"Your son is not of this world!" boomed the ancient voice inside her heart. "He is not reflecting God's image because he does not participate with the world."

"Now I'm really confused!" the woman admitted in her simple way that so attracted people to her side. "What do you mean my son is not of this world so he is not reflecting God's image?"

Everything became quiet—no voice, no thoughts, only the hum of the refrigerator.

"Your son lives to eat," came the voice, deeply penetrating her body, mind, and soul. The refrigerator was like a holy vibration, emanating its hum outwardly for all to feel. "He died a long time ago when you left his father. It broke his heart so much that he swore his life was over. All the hopes he'd had, the ideals he'd based his love on, and his new, everlasting joy were pronounced dead on arrival as you walked out that door. Now he is afraid.

"You talk about burning down the cabin your family built together, and you talk about going to see your ex-husband. The child that died is living in the subconscious buried deep behind the house. If you burn that cabin down there will be no more 'behind the house,' so the man subconsciously thinks there will be no more child buried safely behind the house."

"Complicated!" said the woman, but her interest was sparked with curiosity.

Ever since she was young, she had liked studying the nature of the mind and what made it tick.

That's it! My youngest son also likes to know what makes things tick! He tore apart a clock as a boy and broke his new Etch-a-Sketch, not to be bad but to find out what made it work.

"What will happen to the child buried behind the house if we burn that cabin down?" the lady asked the voice she thought of as God.

"Well, that's easy!" God answered, chirping to her from a bird's mouth right outside her window. "There's a new day coming, a day when families will rejoice. Sons will help their parents, and daughters will support their children and husbands. The strife of the material age is coming to an end."

"Is that why there were price tags on everything in that bed and breakfast I stayed in?" the woman wanted to know.

"No, that's why that bed and breakfast gave you the chance to wake up in the night and smell the stink of alcoholic beverages taking away the duty of the people who consumed them."

"What do you mean?" she asked innocently.

"When a person's duty is taken away by wine, women, or song, there is no more hope left. Duty is at the root of righteousness. When we lose the real thread that binds us together, we have lost our own connection to all that is true, valid, or righteous.

"There were once two singers who called themselves the Righteous Brothers. Many bands and groups came out at the dawning of the new age. These brothers spoke about a bird dying from the loneliness of not being able to find its way out of the prison of worldly existence.

"They were directly speaking the sounds of my direction. Start where you are, continue to walk, and then you end up as a pair of men called the Blue Rodeo singing about trying to overcome addictions. Once that appeals to people, the next phase of life is the Dixie Chicks singing about the loneliness of a girl when the soldier doesn't come home. And finally, a young boy is reborn in prison. He picks up his guitar and begins to sing. He puts away his foolish pride and concentrates on the truth.

"He tells what it was like as a young boy growing up in a cabin of love, and he sings about the heartache that came when his mother left. He begins writing his story, and before long, the parole board wants to speak with him. They want to know his plans for the future, and the boy, newly born again, is very clear. He says in a clear and simple voice, 'I want to tell the truth.' The story continues like this:

The parole officers look at one another and then back at the man sitting in front of them.

"Well, what does that look like?" they ask.

He smiles and looks at his mother and father sitting beside him.

"I want to carry the message of hope to other people. There is no news like good news, so I want to uplift their hopeless lives by being an example. With the support of my parents, I will get together a music studio and play some of this material I've been working on. There is a CD I want to make, and I will take it to a music producer my Father has connections with."

The people on the board look impressed as their eyes turn to the man sitting before them.

"Well, actually, when I said *my Father,* I meant the one in heaven that has restored me to my original self," says the man being questioned. "I'm grateful to my dad for all he did to continue teaching me about music and then neglecting me for so many years. Many people would be bitter, but that's the point of my CD. Bitterness only drives us crazy. Forgiveness is the key that unlocks the success, true success, which is eternal. I want to play music when I get out."

"What about your dream to go to art college?" his professional support team admonishes.

"Oh, I definitely want to go to college," the young man explains. "But that is to gain the experience that was taken away in my youth. I always wanted to be good, to be a source of accomplishment and pride for my parents, but the drug life robbed me of everything beautiful.

"Now I'm a simple person. What my dreams consist of are helping children to realize their dreams and being a support to the community. If all this sounds too good to be true, you will see by my calm demeanor and sincere heart that I'm no con anymore. I believe in the power of a righteous man and the synchronicity of faith. When the two are put together, then out comes a song."

After that day the mother of the boy became very quiet. Her enthusiasm for life seemed to be gone.

"What's the matter, Mom?" asked the boy. "Don't you love me anymore?" he wanted to know.

"The world is a mirror in which God's image reflects," said the woman.

The boy got mad.

"That's such a bunch of bull!" he said. "Talk to me in a regular way!" he retorted. "I'm tired of all that kind of talk. The prophesies ... the superstitions ... the pretend world you live in! Get real!"

His mother began to cry, and he suddenly understood what the problem between them had always been. She'd supported the family, but no one in the family had supported her. She had always been alone, and that was why she had left the cabin life so many years before.

"I'm sorry, Ma," he said. "You can believe me now when I say I'm sorry. You were always there for us. You unselfishly mowed lawns, waitressed for long hours in the evening, and cut fish during the day trying to give us a good place to live and new clothes to wear. You cooked everything from scratch because you love to bake and believed in pure food to help children grow up with healthy bodies and minds.

"You tried to get us to look at ourselves, prophesied the bad omens when your loved ones were threatened, and studied the lives of the spiritual masters because you knew, they knew, the way to help your family and friends was with a pure heart.

"You quit drugs because you saw the bad effects on your family. You spent countless hours, breaking all of your habits and sleep routine, to help the world by writing your story. You moved far from home and walked miles through sun, rain, and snowstorms, trying to encourage me to be a good person, and now I yell at *you* to get real? I'm really sorry," he said.

"I'm going to prove my words," he went on. "You taught me that. To prove by my actions to be all that I can be and not just keep saying I'm sorry. You're going to see a changed man from now on. I will work those same steps you worked when you got clean from drugs. I will let go of the macho-bully image that always got me into trouble, and I will ask for help from my elders and people I admire."

The woman smiled as the boy who was now a man wiped away her tears. These were not ordinary promises; these words had strength. She began to talk, and for once, the boy opened his mind completely to what she had to say. He was no longer seeing her as some phony prophet, misguiding people through spiritual ravings or the exhortations of a crazy mother.

At last, he saw who she truly was, a silent monk in a woman's body. Her guru's love was complete and unwavering. Something like a current waved through him, and lights began to flash in his mind. His mother had been helping him all along the way, and now he was determined to cooperate.

"The world is a mirror that reflects God's image," he began to write, as he completed the assignment his mother had given so many years before back in the cabin.

"Please do your homework son," she'd pleaded, but he hadn't listened. Now things were changing. He had finally begun to listen.

CHAPTER 3

God Will Show the Way

THE CRAZY WOMAN WAS NOW gone from the young man's sights, and before him sat someone he could trust.

"I'm going to open a shelter for victims," his mother said when he looked her way.

She didn't know how she would do it, but she was sure that God would show her the way.

"How will you find the money?" her son asked, and the woman started to laugh.

"Why, the money is not lost!" she said.

He felt humbled by her joke but didn't mind anymore. He had nothing left to prove to anyone. He knew he was loved and safe just being the person he was.

"What about your wrist, Ma?" he asked in a way familiar to only the two of them.

Her wrist had been sore for quite some time. The young man was concerned, for he loved his mother and felt her pain as his very own.

"I don't know about that," she said, "but I suspect several things are happening, based on my experiences in the past."

Now that his mind had opened, the man wanted to know more.

"Well, over the years this little body took on the misdeeds of others so it could pass along goodness instead."

"What do you mean?" he asked.

"There was once a woman whose foot was so sore she couldn't walk. She'd been invited to my yoga class and was drinking a glass of wine at her kitchen table when we finally had the chance to speak."

"What happened?" he asked.

"Well, I saw that the woman had a sincere heart but was masking her true condition in order to escape going to class."

"That doesn't make sense!" he thought aloud, for now there was no more hiding from his mom.

"Well, she was actually an alcoholic," said his mother, who was unafraid of the truth.

"So what did that have to do with her foot and the yoga class?"

"The woman felt very inferior in her town, so she went to great lengths to prove to everyone what a rich and powerful person she was. She opened a small restaurant in the village and had all kinds of delicacies brought in to the demise of her own well-being. The people in the town laughed behind her back, saying she was wearing pants too big for the little woman she was.

"Feeling their negativity, the woman got even more determined. 'I'll show them!' she said, and she began to remodel her house. She made the mistake of hiring one of the local men, who gave the inside story of all her business affairs to everyone in the small village. It seemed the rich and powerful woman could do nothing right.

"Then one day she got a phone call from a woman wanting to work for her. Since her restaurant was now closed, she had begun a new business, teaching English as a second language. The woman applying for the job was new in town and was trying to find her way until she could get employment in her own field."

"Hey! That woman was you!" the young man smiled, anticipating a great turn of events in the small-town woman's life.

"Well, yes," his mother said. "I phoned her after a friend gave me her number. She said she desperately needed someone right away, and we agreed to meet. After a short interview, I got the job and did very well. Since the woman lived near the prison you were in at the time, she offered me a place to stay when I came to visit."

"So what does all this have to do with healing and taking on people's hurts?" he asked.

"I came to her village one night to teach a yoga class. The language, if you recall, was mainly French, and I needed a translator."

"You two were really working together with languages, huh, Ma?" he said rather sweetly.

"Or so it would seem," the woman said rather shyly.

She did not like to reveal the true nature of her work lest she break the energy. The young man thought his mother had gotten off track. *Perhaps her mind is wandering*, he considered, and then he realized his own problem.

Either I trust or I don't, he decided, and he sat patiently waiting to hear the moral of the story.

Ever since his mother was a child, she liked to read books with a moral. Now her stories were of that same ilk. She sat quietly for a few minutes as though reflecting on some past event.

"That woman was very brave," she continued. "She had a daughter she was determined to raise with culture, education, and pomp."

"Pomp?" asked the son. "That sounds old-fashioned!"

"Well, I think the lady was a queen somewhere along the line. She had very royal blood and even found pleasure displaying a Crown Royal box on top of her china cabinet. Everyone else thought it was about whiskey, but she knew differently!"

"So, what about your wrist?" he asked, getting a bit impatient.

"Oh, yes. Now the wrist was decisively an attempt to release her from the shackles she wore around her ankles."

"What? How does *that* relate to *your* wrist?"

He thought that his mother was pulling his leg as she had a great sense of humor.

"Well, the wrist and the ankle are very similar, you know," she said in all seriousness.

Just then a huge formation of geese flew over. Outside their window, they could hear the gaggle as its V-formation drew energy from the leader.

"The geese have a lot to teach us, son, as does all of nature. When geese fly in formation, they are making a tunnel of wind—a current, if you like—that pulls the others behind the main goose flying in the lead role."

"Yes," he said. "And if one gets hurt and drops down, another goose will drop out of formation to stay with the wounded one until it either dies or gets well enough to fly with another flock."

"Yes!" said his mom. "Where did you hear that?"

"You told me we remind you of the geese and that you dropped out of society to stay by my side until I could fly again."

"Or be killed," she said, looking very sad.

"Oh, don't say that!" It was the boy's turn to scold his mother. "Please, Mom, don't put fears in my head."

"No, son," she said. "You don't understand. I repeat what I see just like a little child. You have the fear that you will be killed. If we don't hide our fears but talk about them openly, it dissipates the energy."

"Okay, but sometimes you freak me out!"

"Good. Tell me about that!"

The woman and her son spoke all afternoon until finally he said, "Hey! Wait a minute! You never did finish your story!"

"Oh, yes I did, son. You see, when you began telling me about your fears, the pain in my wrist went away. When the woman told me about her sore foot, it wasn't long before she started walking. Minutes later, she went to hobble to the kitchen for another glass of wine, and she said, "Hey! The pain in my foot is gone!'

"Great!" I told her. "Now you can come translate for me in the yoga class!"

"Now I'm all confused," said the aging boy, for he still thought of himself as a boy after so many years of being deprived of his true and rightful place in the community.

"Confused about what?"

The mom looked at him innocently, but there was a twinkle in her eye.

"This story wasn't about that woman at all, was it?" he asked.

"Oh yes!" she replied. "That woman was very important to me, and still is," said the lady, flicking a piece of dust off of her white dress.

"Well, what did her hurt have to do with your wrist? And why does my talking about my fears make the pain go away?"

"That's easy in theory, son, but until you experience something yourself, you just have to trust your elders who know the truth."

"I trust you now more than ever before," he said.

"Yes, but there's still a shadow of doubt," she said, understanding how hard it is to let go completely for fear of trust being broken … again. "The pain in my wrist came from the judgment of the community, like when the women back in the olden days had to wear the scarlet letter A for *adultery* so the whole community would mock them."

"You mean this woman was an adulteress?" he asked.

"Listen, son. If we follow the precepts of righteousness as handed down through the ages by the masters of spirituality, we will see that all of us create a vacuum of evil when we refuse to live correctly. In English, the word *evil* spells *live* backward, denoting exactly what will come from wrong and neglectful actions."

"So?" he asked.

"So the woman didn't like being judged by the people in her community, but she judged *them* even more harshly."

"How so?"

"She didn't like the simple way they dressed, and many were uneducated and knew nothing of culture and pomp— everything she lived to bring forward in her mediocre life."

"And what did that have to do with you?"

"Well, I appeared at her doorstep many times to give her the opportunity to serve the poor instead of judge them. She wanted to smoke in her house but knew I would not be able to handle it, so she began hiding her cigarettes until I was gone. She was used to drinking alone at night once her daughter was in bed, but when I was there, she became uncomfortable. The meat she cooked became bloody and violent in my presence, and her pomp and false set of glamour rules were displayed openly for her to see.

"After a month or two, she began making excuses why I couldn't stay there anymore, saying the prison officials were more important. She said she couldn't risk losing her teaching contract by keeping the mother of a murderer in her home. From the very beginning, she asked me about her spirituality, and eventually she joined a fellowship for recovering alcoholics. When they wanted to be a part of her life, she became determined to keep to herself and eventually quit going."

"*And your wrist?*" he asked as though he would pop.

"Well, my wrist gathered up all her pomp, arrogance, and self-pity. It began to fester inside waiting for someone like you to release it."

"Someone like me?"

"Yes," she said. "It kind of works like magic, but in all actuality there is no magic to it. It's purely scientific!"

"Oh, yes!" he said, getting a wee bit sarcastic for he was getting tired, and whenever he got tired, his old ways still slipped out. "Hungry, angry, lonely, or tired spells *halt!*" his parole officer at the old institution had warned.

"The rule of cause and effect will not be forsaken," she went on. "It reminds me of Jesus crying out, 'Oh God, why hath Thou forsaken me?' while hanging on the cross."

"That was pretty sad," said the man.

"Well, actually it was, and *is* just like that," said the woman. "Jesus called out to God, but what he called out was actually the main error that caused all the suffering in the first place. One massive remark came bolting from his lips, but know it to be certain, that thought was not his. He was releasing for the people their sinful way of thinking, and now, by your telling me all about your fears, I am releasing the pain of that lady's judgment on the lesser people, or as she saw it, the scum of society."

"Gee, thanks," said the man, but there was a smile on his face, for now he understood the way to love. "Sometimes we need to sacrifice, right?" he asked. "Our health, our money, and our comfort, in order to help others."

"Yes," smiled his mom, for she was happy that her son was finally listening.

CHAPTER 4

Where There Is Dharma,
There Is Victory

THE NEXT TIME THE WOMAN saw her son, he was a changed man. He'd shaved his head, and his meditation mat was pulled out of the closet. He was ready to pick up where he'd left off nearly a year before. There was a celebration coming in his life, and he was looking forward to the milestone but wasn't quite sure why.

He thought, *What will it be but one more day?* And then he remembered his uncle's famous words for people recovering from drug addiction: "When it comes your day to celebrate, take it for all it is worth," he had said with a grin. "Whether it's 1 day, 30 days, 60 days, 90 days, three months, or a year clean, take that plastic chip the fellowship offers like it's a piece of gold because you earned it one day at a time."

The man's thoughts came back to the small cell he'd lived in for over thirteen years. He didn't so much mind the toilet being in the same room as his bed. Why, some cheap motels offer the same accommodations.

The things that matter to me the most are my family, he thought. *I want to see my sister's children as they grow, and I want to participate in their lives. I want to admire the work my father does on motorcycles and eat my mother's cooking. Working nine to five doesn't frighten me, and paying taxes will be a privilege. I just want to go home.*

Hmmm … that word, *home*. It reminded him of the word his mother had so often encouraged him to repeat over and over in his mind. She called it *japa* and showed him how to count on a string of 108 beads from India called a *japa mala*.

Those gods and goddesses she prays to will be obsolete when she realizes the superstition, he mused. Once again he quickly bit the tongue of his thoughts. *I trust my mom,* he remembered, refusing to let the old negative thoughts get entangled with the good he was trying to do.

He called his mother that night and asked her to repeat one of the mantras, saying he really wanted to get stronger spiritually.

"That's easy, son," she said. "You are a man who loves family, and the Bhagavad Gita recommends that we follow our dharma. Where there is dharma, there is victory. You can bet on that!"

"Well, I've sure appreciated all you've done for me," he said.

"That's victorious!" she said. "You told me not to come in the beginning, and your attitude toward the guards was less than personable!"

He laughed, remembering the time she had him spit out his gum and throw it in the trash instead of on the table.

"It's the screw's job to clean it up!" he had said with an angry scowl.

"Well, I was angry," he told her. "Real angry."

"About what?"

"If I tell you, do you promise not to get mad?"

"Yes, I promise," his mother vowed, preparing herself for the blame that was surely on its way.

"I was angry that you left Dad."

"I know," she said.

"And then you went out with other losers who were twice as bad as him!"

"That's comparing," she said. "Try hard not to do that."

"And there—you're always giving me advice," he said. "Do you know how that makes me feel?"

"No, son. Please tell me. I'm open to hearing what you have to say."

"Yeah, right!" he said. "Then you'll be mad, and I have to feel guilty."

"No, you don't have to feel guilty. You'll ..." but then the woman stopped.

She paused before falling into the same old trap.

"If you want me to be angry, you're going to have to work a lot harder than that!" she finally said.

"What?" he said, as though she'd dumped cold water on his head.

"I said you can't make me do anything. I want to make that real clear. And I can't make you do anything either. If I give advice, it's because I care. You, on the other hand, can say thank you or throw the advice in the trash. I do it all the time," she said with a laugh.

"What's that supposed to mean?" he asked. "You throw my advice in the trash?"

"Sure," she said. "Do you know what it's been like all these years living with cons?"

She didn't give him a chance to jump in before she continued.

"I love you, but I must admit, you need to give your head a shake."

The words fell from her mouth before she had a chance to feel out her son's response.

"I come to the prison to visit you, and I can't look at anyone. I'm not supposed to be friendly, which is my natural disposition. You tell me, 'Do this, don't do that.' Even when you say I make you feel guilty, it feels like an attempt to control me. You play on my emotions with loving remarks and then threaten to escape by killing yourself. Do you know how a mother would feel with news like that? She goes home and she wonders. *Is he okay? Did I say something to upset him?* Well, let me tell you son—*that makes me angry!*"

He looked surprised. He hadn't seen his mother act this way before, and he was taken aback.

She looks kind of cute when she's angry, he thought, but he knew she'd flip her lid if he said something like that.

"So what else makes you angry?" he asked, reversing the roles for a minute or two.

"Well, if you must know, I get angry with all the secrets in our family. When I talk with one person, it's about the other, and when I talk with the other, it's about someone else."

"You do it too."

"Me included! And that makes me feel angry! I don't want to pretend, I don't want to lie, and I'm darned tootin' gonna be myself, no matter what anyone thinks!"

"Is that all?"

"I guess so," she smiled. "Yes, that's all."

"Darn tootin', huh?"

"And don't make fun of me! That makes me angry!" she cried as a slight smile formed on her rarely stern lips.

"I'll try to remember all that," he said. "Now do you want to hear more about my anger?"

"Sure," she smiled. "That felt great expressing it—not needing to fight, but just expressing it."

"And if it doesn't change?" he asked with a smirk.

"I'm gonna wear purple sneakers, a green jogging suit two sizes too small, and a big felt hat with plastic yellow flowers the next time I come to the prison to visit you!"

They both laughed and carried on for quite a while, and then her son looked very serious.

"You know what really does make me feel angry, Mom?"

"No, son. Please, tell me," she said with every bit of kindness she had stored up inside.

He looked around a few times and then whispered in her ear. She was shocked by the language he used but knew he had to talk freely in order to release all the stagnant energy he'd held inside for so many years. Everything was monitored, filmed, and recorded. He had no privacy, and now one simple whisper in his mother's ear seemed to release a lifetime of upset.

"Is that what's been bothering you all these years?" she asked.

"Yes," he said, looking rather sheepish.

"Well, son, I want you to know, those carob bunnies I made for you kids that Easter fell down behind the shelf under the curtain where I was keeping them cool until Easter morning. I'm sorry I accused you of taking them, but you were always into things, and I really thought you did it."

"And another thing," he said, and he whispered once more in her ear.

"I'm not trying to say you accused me of that, but the letters you write sometimes, channeled or not, are real confusing to me. Where do they come from, and why don't you just write in your regular way?"

"I'll try to explain in as simple a way as I can."

"Don't insult me, now," he said, sitting up. "I am, after all, Amarnath, the great one!" He had a teasing smile.

"That Sanskrit name came to you from my guru," she said, wanting her son to take it seriously. "He's a spiritual master who knows the wound as well as the star in every person that comes to him for protection.

"Now, to answer your question, I read a book a long time ago about Edgar Cayce," she said, trying to explain what she called channeled letters. "He was called the Sleeping Prophet because he could see inside people by going into a sleep-like trance. I read about his life as a young teen, and somehow I knew that I too, could see inside people. I wanted to be just like Edgar Cayce when I grew up, helping people to understand the root of their problems and offering support for their healing."

"Yes, and the letters? What about those?"

"Well, that's my way," explained his mother. "I get still and listen, and the guidance comes."

"But what if the guidance is wrong?" he asked.

"It's not wrong, but sometimes people have lessons to learn. I've been tested many times because I had to look at my arrogance, fear, or impatience."

"Maybe you should write a letter for me, now that I'm able to hear it."

"Maybe you should ask!" she scolded, without being cruel. "When you ask, the guidance flows more freely."

"I ask a lot when you're not listening," he said very humbly, almost shy.

She started to remember what he had been like a long time ago, before she'd begun leaving his father in her mind.

"I used to love your dad," she said.

"I know," he remarked rather sadly.

"No, I don't think you do. I mean I used to be able to love your dad without condition. I'd look in the mirror wanting to be pretty for him, and I'd run out to meet him at the end of our driveway when he came home from school or work. But something changed between us, and I'm not sure when."

"It was when I was born," said her son, with a hint of sadness.

"What?" she asked.

"One time Dad said, 'Your mother used to be mine until you came along. Ever since then she's been more concerned with you!'"

The look and the tone of voice displayed by her son broke her heart, but she didn't say so.

"Well, he was absolutely correct," she said. "And that's my fault, not yours. You were an innocent baby. I doted on you, thought you were everything, and let myself go concerning the make-up of a husband and wife's sexuality."

"I don't want to hear more," the boy said. "I get all weird when my parents talk about sex."

"That's natural," his mother assured him.

"It is?" He was surprised.

"Of course," she said. "You don't need details, but you do need to know one thing."

"What?" he asked.

"You're not gay," she laughed.

"That's not funny!" he said, looking around.

"No, I mean it. And you don't ever have to prove it to anyone. I know people will talk and wonder what happens to people when they go to prison for so many years, but your business is your own. If you are kind to people and you love children the way you wanted to be loved, you will be just fine."

All of a sudden, the bell for shift change sounded, and the boy sat up.

"Whew!" he said. "That was heavy! I feel like I was in a dark tunnel buried deep beneath the ground."

"You were," said his mom. "I'm going to see your father. The two of us are going to burn that old cabin down and …"

"And what?" he asked.

"Oh, nothing," she said.

"Hey, wait a minute! You can't just leave without finishing your sentence," he said. "And what?"

"Oh, I'll tell you tomorrow. There's not enough time now, and besides, you'll think I'm silly."

"Well, that wouldn't be the first time!" The young man smiled as he walked his mom to the door. "See you tomorrow, Mom," he said.

"Okay," she said.

"I love you," he called.

"Love you too," she said, and the steel door slammed shut behind her.

CHAPTER 5

To Wonder Is to Blunder

W HEN THE MOTHER GOT TO the door, something strange
happened. It was as if the key to unlock the prison door
was right inside her heart; all she had to do was turn it.

Hmmm, she thought, walking out with the other visitors,
who were mostly women. Very rarely did male visitors come
to these institutions. She began to wonder why, and then she
remembered her teacher's words of wisdom.

"To wonder is to blunder," he'd said, with his unusual grin
that could light up a whole room.

Now why would he say a thing like that? she wondered, not
realizing she'd just done it again.

She'd been writing her life story, hoping to help even one
person to get through their hard times with a little more peace
than she'd had. Once in a while she'd meet a stumbling block,
but not very often. Writing and sewing seemed to come easy to
her; she didn't mind sitting for long hours to put together pen

and paper or needle and thread. She hoped for the best and just got going. Whoever knew what would come of her work? She suddenly pictured the beautiful young man so aspiring to do well in life sitting behind the dreary prison walls.

Wow, she thought. *He is truly amazing! How could any person so sweet as a child turn so violent and then return to being sweet?* But there she was, wondering again. The theme of her book should be about wonders instead of miracles!

Now I'm really going beyond the beyond, she thought with a silent chuckle. *Hmmm, to wonder is to blunder. I don't understand that at all, but my teacher's words always hold some essence of truth that is slowly revealed.*

She suddenly remembered the last sentence she was about to tell her son.

He's not prepared for this, she thought. *Even Krishna's devotees were shocked when he left his monk's clothing in the forest, donned fine robes, and got married. What would my simple life look like if I were to accept the role of wife again and remarry my ex-husband?*

The boy she called son had grown up, and her daughter had three children of her own. She was glad that her eldest son's country craft store was a success, but still, she was not happy.

Where is the family unit? she questioned. *One person here, one person there. If someone gets sick, married, or divorced, where is the tight support of community?*

The woman wondered again and again of these complex problems until, finally, she was sure she would find the truth!

One of her secret dreams was to build a good home where people pitch in and help one another. She didn't know that the house was already built. She just had to show up and play her part, and all else would follow. Too unsure of the outcome to let things flow naturally, she decided to make something happen.

What would my ex-husband do if I just appeared on his doorstep? Maybe he wouldn't talk to me or maybe he would say, "Go away!" Well, I'll just sit there making certain he will talk to me, she thought. And then, *No, that wouldn't be right. He lives with another woman!*

And so it went. One day she was going to build a house, but she didn't know how the money would come. The next day she was sure—she *would* have a house to bring the family all together again. Whenever her mind weakened, it filled with the deeply ingrained doubts of her childhood when she had no parents to support her.

Why don't we all move to British Columbia? she considered, and then she remembered her father's words of wisdom: "It is not right to figure out other people's lives, any more than you would want them to figure out yours."

God, she prayed from deep within her heart, *here is the last thing I was going to say to my son. I was going to tell him that I was going to see his father, and the two of us were going to burn that old cabin down. I was about to say I hoped he would come live with us and make a family together the way the Waltons[1] did. But the bell rang for a shift change, and I had to leave while he went back to his cell.*

The lady felt vulnerable being honest with God because her ideas seemed silly sometimes. She was a simple person who believed in miracles. She wanted to stay close with her children even when they weren't in trouble. She believed that grandchildren needed support from their grandparents, and heaven knows that parents *can* use a break sometimes! Enjoying nature, relaxing into the flow of life, and supporting all things

---

[1] *The Waltons:* An American television series (1971-1981) based on the book *Spencer's Mountain*

loving and kind were what she felt to be important. She knew the world could flourish if people only took what they needed and passed on the very best of what they had to offer, not just the remains of what they didn't like.

I wonder if my son would want that. He often says he's happy with family, but I wonder if he just says that to be nice.

"To wonder is to blunder!" came the voice again.

Wow! I finally get it, she thought. *Just take things at face value. If we find we can't get along, then we'll change things when the time comes.*

The woman began feeling kind of old.

What if my ex-husband doesn't think I'm pretty anymore? He used to really like pretty women.... What am I thinking? she scolded herself. *He's with someone else!*

But deep inside her heart, she could feel her ex-husband's love. She knew that over all the years, he'd never stopped loving her, and she had never stopped loving him.

Well, maybe by my example, my children will follow their hearts, she thought. *If I don't pursue my dreams, how can I ask them to pursue theirs? I'd be a hypocrite!*

The woman went to town and bought a tent. She borrowed a sleeping bag and had it cleaned for her trip. She didn't like the thought of sleeping in someone else's bedding, but money was scarce, and she had to make do.

I wonder why money is always scarce for poor people and rich people always have more than enough? Maybe it is how they think! That's it! To wonder is to blunder! You've got to know!

After returning the cleaned sleeping bag, she invested her money in a brand new one. She got a larger pack and prepared for the long journey ahead.

Maybe I'll walk like the Peace Pilgrim did, she joked, but deep inside she'd always wanted to do something like that. Her faith was getting stronger, and she lived for the day she could be still and "know that I am God."

That must really be something, she thought, *being still and knowing God within all creatures. That's what I'll do! When I get to my ex-husband's doorstep, I'll just be still and know that I am God! If I am God, then he also is God when he is still. I won't pressure him for anything but ask if we can go for a walk. If he agrees, then the God in him is equal to the God in me, and there will be harmony between us.*

The woman put all thoughts out of her mind.

"To wonder is to blunder," she said firmly, as she walked to catch the early morning bus to the prison.

CHAPTER 6

Let There Be Light

A STRANGER CAME TO TOWN one day, and the woman was very happy to see him.

"Let there be light!" he'd say, and "This is all God's amazing grace!"

She didn't know who he was, but he was very serene like Jesus, and he loved little children. He seemed firm in his faith, and he didn't worry about what people thought of him.

"That's one of my biggest problems," she told the man. "I worry about what people will think, and I often stay quiet when the truth should be told."

He looked her right in the eye and said, "Oh, I don't think that's the truth at all. I think you've been listening to other people doubt themselves, so you're feeling like you *should* doubt yourself. That's finished for you. The firmness of your faith has been in place a long time."

"Well, maybe I'm messing with powers that come through practicing yoga postures and breathing techniques."

"Were you seeking power when you began?" he asked.

"No, I was seeking the ability to love without condition. I wanted to be pure like Jesus was with little children. Even with his enemies he never showed maliciousness concerning his spirituality."

"Why don't you ask yourself a couple of questions?" the man advised. "If the answer is yes, then give up what you're doing completely, for only evil will come when the ego gets involved."

"What do you mean?"

"You spoke about powers. Number one, can you never use them again without a blink of the eye?"

"Oh, yes," said the woman. "If a spiritual master said, 'Don't ever do that again,' I would drop it completely from my life."

"Okay, and number two, do you want people's respect for how powerful you are?"

"Well, that's what I'm not so sure about. Maybe I do because I know it's the love of God, and the guidance I receive is so pure and helpful. It's like giving a fine-cut jewel to someone who is very poor, saying, 'If you take this jewel and sell it in the marketplace, you will make enough money to feed your family and keep them warm for two years.' Then, when they walk away, they say, 'Yeah right, lady,' and toss the emerald into the bushes."

"So you don't really want respect for yourself; it's for the teachings?"

"Well, yes, I guess so," she said, beginning to feel a little better.

She was happy to be an instrument of God's blessings and didn't really want to stop. It gave her purpose, kind of like the old saying, "If you give a man a fish, you feed him for a day; if you teach a man to fish, you feed him for a lifetime."

"Know that all is well," said the kind stranger.

She felt like she'd known him a very long time.

Well, maybe in another lifetime, she thought, and as he walked away, she had an idea.

"Excuse me," she said, running after him. "Do you know me?"

He looked at her for a few minutes and then smiled.

"Yes, I know you," he said. "But if you don't remember me, it's okay."

He walked with a bit of a limp, and there seemed to be a trace of sadness in how he looked at the world.

"Excuse me," she said running after him again. "You are so kind; you make me want to stay with you."

"No, that isn't necessary," he said. "You go help the world and know that whenever you need me, all you need to do is picture my kindness. We often place value on a face or the physical appearance of a person, but what you are really in love with is the principle."

"I don't know if I understand," she said.

"You understand," he said. "We have worked together before, and we'll work together again, but for now, you have a mission. I just stopped into town to help you get going. We knew you were beginning to falter by the light emanations coming from your being."

"What do you mean?"

"Well, as one realizes the Truth they are very close to becoming one with the divinity within themselves. It is very hard at the last level because most people cannot relate to purity and goodness, and they begin to persecute the person. If the person buys into the persecution, their light begins to fade, and their auric field gets weak."

"What should a person do if that starts to happen?" she asked.

"Let there be light!" he said with a smile, and he walked up the road.

The woman didn't feel like chasing him, but instead, she felt warm inside—calm as though she were one of the sun's rays.

"Let there be light!" she said, and she walked home to make supper.

CHAPTER 7

Do Your Own Mission

THE WOMAN FELT RATHER DEJECTED one morning. She'd written to her stepmother saying thank you for all the lessons she'd taught her through both her good actions and her bad. When her stepmom didn't reply, she decided she was tired of being neglected. In the past, she'd tried very hard to please her, thinking, *If only I can love her enough, she will certainly begin showing me some affection.* But many years passed, and nothing—no card, no letters, only a phone call when the woman thought she was dying. In fact, many people called and came to see her when they thought she was dying.

What's with this? she wondered. *Maybe I do too much to please people. Maybe I shouldn't care so much.*

Then she remembered the stranger's words.

"You have a mission," he said. "Just do your own mission. Other people also have what we call an assignment in life, much the same as kids with homework in school. If they do their assignment, they pass to the next level.

"Your stepmother's assignment was to leave you to suffer from the degeneration of your sins from the past. It has not been easy, this role she took, but it was the best one suited to her cold nature.

"We match the actor with the act. When an actor is able to walk on the stage of life and do their duty without desiring fame, wealth, or being attached to the results in any way, they have passed their testing ground and can move to the next level of enlightenment."

"That must have been hard for her all these years!" said the woman. "I always felt like she loved me but that something was holding us apart. She'd tell me I was a good person when she'd see me almost as though she wasn't supposed to."

"She wasn't," he told her. "There was supposed to be no contact with you in the form of encouragement or love. She was to remain cold and unconcerned, but she couldn't hold up. Your brother John was also to rely on your strength to be good and not depend on a parent's love. You faltered a few times, but that was to be expected. You had a huge debt to pay."

The woman felt kind of uneasy with this information.

What do I do now? she wondered, but the telephone rang and distracted her pondering.

"Hello?" she said, wondering who could be calling so early in the morning.

"It's me!" said a rather shy, young voice.

"Me?" asked the woman.

"Yes, I'm an old friend of yours named Cyndy. We used to go to school together until you graduated and left me behind."

"Oh, well, it's good to hear from you," said the woman, bewildered at why, after so many years, this girl, who was now a grown woman, would be contacting her.

"Well, I have some things I'd really like to set straight," said Cyndy. "First of all, I always hated the way you called me Minnie instead of my real name, Cyndy. I didn't like being so skinny, as you well knew, and that name drove me to anger."

"I'm sorry," said the woman. "Anything else?"

"Yes, the way you took my mother's attention really pissed me off, if you'll pardon the expression."

"Go ahead," said the woman.

She could see the lady really needed to unload some old feelings that she had kept locked up as resentments.

"I have one or two good things to say also," she said, "but those can wait. If I don't get this other stuff off my chest, I think I'll burst! I was glad to get your phone number and really hope you can hear me to the end."

"Yes, certainly," offered the woman.

"There was a time I looked up to you as an older person. You seemed intelligent and pretty, and I thought I wanted to be just like you one day."

"Oh," said the woman, not daring to break her courage.

"When you graduated from high school, you forgot all about me. I tried to hang around with you, but when you introduced me as Minnie, I felt as small as a mouse and my anger as big as a lion."

"Well, can I do anything to help set all of this straight?" the woman asked.

"No, but you can let me finish."

"Okay," said the woman, still puzzled by this unexpected phone call.

Cyndy went on for over half an hour saying things about their childhood that the woman had completely forgotten, and then suddenly she went quiet.

"Is there more?" the woman asked, but Cyndy had begun to cry.

"I miss you with all my heart," she said. "I would give anything to hear you call out, 'Hey Min', c'mon over!'"

This was a strange turn of events! The woman listened while Cyndy went on to say all the positive results their relationship had brought, and then she went quiet again.

"Is it true your youngest son is in prison and has been there for many years?"

"Yes," said the woman, "but he is doing just fine. He got in trouble as a result of many wrong turns he took as a youth. Now he is returning from those crossroads and making choices more conducive to the well-being of many people."

"Can I have a picture of you?" Cyndy asked.

"I guess so," said the woman. "Do you need a new dartboard?"

Cyndy laughed, saying her mom really thought the woman would have made a good nurse.

"Yes, she tried to get me to go on to nursing school," said the woman. "But I too was pretty confused at that time. The people I looked up to were drinking and taking drugs. Through my own resentments, I followed their way of life, forgetting all things and people like you in my life that were beautiful and loving."

"Beautiful?" Cyndy said, her voice sounding like that of a fifteen-year-old girl.

"Yes, beautiful. Remember when I cut my hair real short that time? I was emulating you. I thought you were extremely hilarious, and as you developed, I was happy to see how beautiful you turned out."

"Even with my big nose?" she asked.

"Yes, even with your special features. You had class and knew how to dress. The furniture in your room and the way you took care of the kids made me proud to be your friend."

"My furniture?"

"Yes, you were so respectful of your grandmother and often spoke about the way she taught you to antique your furniture with gold paint."

Cyndy started to laugh. "I still do that," she said.

They talked a long time until finally the woman said, "I am really glad you got up the courage to call."

Cyndy thanked the woman for her loving kindness, and the two parted ways, saying good-bye like the best of friends. And so they were.

CHAPTER 8

Tell the Truth

ONE EVENING, THE WOMAN GOT another phone call. She was beginning to show signs of age, her son noticed, and he wondered if she thought he was too. When she picked up the phone, he didn't start with his usual, "Hi, Mom," but said, "Namasté![2] I was thinking of you so thought I'd better call."

"Well, that's great," said the woman, pleased to hear him using spiritual language.

She could always tell what was on his mind by the kind of words he used. When he was small, he had liked the song "I's the B'y that Catches Flies, and I's the B'y that Eats Them!" He'd sing that song and then laugh until he was red in the face. Then he began to change his words into more frustrating ones like "I

---

[2] Namaste: A Hindu greeting meaning, "The divine in me recognizes the divine in you."

don't know" and "Whatever!" As he grew some more, he used swear words and said, "Who cares?" a lot, and finally, when he went to prison, he asked, "Do you still love me?"

"I don't know why I'm calling tonight," he said, "I just feel kind of lonely."

"Me too," said his mother. "The loneliness will not go away until I see you walk free," she explained.

"Are you sitting down?" he asked.

"Oh, son, don't ask me that. I used to think you were teasing when you'd ask that and then would really give me good news instead of bad, but no, you never did."

"Are you sitting down?" he said again.

She heard something in his voice that she hadn't heard for a long, long time. When he was a young boy, he'd received a prize for writing the best story in his class. He got all dressed up in his gray suit pants and wore a matching shirt and tie to receive the gift his class offered at the end-of-the-year award ceremony.

"Mom?" he said quietly.

The tone of his voice was the same as that day he'd told her he was getting presented with class honors.

"What, son?" she asked, trying not to get too excited, for the prison way of life had its ups and downs. One day's exciting news could be broken real easy by a guard's decision to change the prisoner's life forever.

"We're going to have our dream come true!"

"What do you mean, son?" she asked, not wanting hope to crush her again.

She had once believed in her dreams. The cabin in the woods with her family had been a long time coming. They had worked so hard to make that dream come true, and then—smash—down it went.

"Mom," he said evenly, in an attempt to control his excitement, "the parole board meets next month, and the officer in charge of my case wants you and Dad to come."

"Well, son, you know I'll be there, but I cannot say for certain that your dad will."

"Mom, I just want you to know that Dad will come if you ask him. Please go bring him here. Please?"

"I have wanted to talk with him, so maybe this will be a good time to do so. Did I ever tell you your father was also a writer?"

"No, but I'm not too surprised. What a talented person he is, and most of those talents have gone unappreciated."

"The best we can do is to appreciate him today and hope he knows the love we have always held in our hearts for him."

"Will you go, Mom? I really need you both here for the parole hearing."

"Yes, son. You know there is nothing I wouldn't do to help you come home."

"Mom, you know that Andy doll you made for me when I was a small boy?"

"Yes," she said, feeling a sense of endearment that her son remembered.

"I loved that doll."

"I know, son. I was always so pleased that you accepted my gift and loved it so much."

"And you know what else?"

"No, son. What?" she asked, unsure of where all of this was leading.

"I'm really glad you taught me that ritual of waving the lights and tossing water over our shoulders."

"Okay, son, that's nice," said his mother.

"And you know what else?"

"No, dear. What?"

"Well, I'm thinking that if you join me when I get out and we have an art studio together, it won't work very well."

"Oh," she said. "Why not?"

"Because you always end up the leader, and I need to feel important. I want it to be my thing with young people. No offense, Mom, but you're getting old, and we still want to be young."

"I know, son. The years have had their way with this poor little body."

"Don't talk like that, Mum," he said, reverting back to his familiar way of speaking.

"Well, you know what I was thinking recently?" she said.

"No, what?"

"I too thought about us working together and remembered the time I started doing stained glass. Your dad had his guitar to play, and he was very good at that. People loved his woodwork, and he could build houses and boats and fix cars."

"But he didn't earn very much money," said her son.

"Earning money is actually a sign of devotion."

"Devotion?" he asked.

"Yes, to your wife, family, country, or God."

"But what if you have no devotion?" asked the young man, who was beginning to feel old.

"Well, devotion is the key that unlocks success. When you earn money with the thought of being rich or using it to harm others, it will not last long in your life. When you use it as the means to uplift the consciousness of several people, then all abundance begins to flow."

He was always interested when his mom spoke about money because he knew that she knew. She never seemed broke anymore. Maybe she was no millionaire, but she always used her money to give others a chance at healing.

"Son, do me a favor, will you?"

"Okay, sure," he said without hesitation.

"When you get out, pick me a rose from the old flower garden where I used to work when I first began bringing money home to feed and clothe our family."

"Okay," he said.

"Do not tell anyone what you're doing, but go to the ocean, and tell God you want to be a good and honest person!"

"I *am* a good and honest person!" he said.

"Yes, but when you get out of prison, many temptations will come your way. If you do as I ask, your heart will be purified so that when those allurements come, you will be strong enough to walk away."

"Okay," he said. "But, Mom?"

"Yes, son?"

"Will you let me have my own art gallery without sharing the space with your stained glass?"

"As I was saying earlier, your dad was so talented that I admired everything he did. I was pleased for his accomplishments, but when I decided to make stained glass windows, he wanted to do it also. I knew he could do anything well, and everyone was always charmed by his presence. I often felt useless just cleaning the house and cooking. I needed something of my own to help me feel important."

"Yeah, I can understand," said the son. "So what did you do?"

"I told him the truth. 'This is my thing!' I blurted out one day. My words and emotions were pretty turbulent at that time," she said. "Actually, I wanted to talk to you about something also."

"What's that?" he asked.

"I've missed you so much over the years. Do you think it would be possible for us to live together on the same piece of land? We could have our own homes but still do things together."

He laughed. "You know what, Ma?" he said. "I really enjoy being with you too. We're birds of a feather, and we stick together!"

"Yeah, like geese!" she said.

"Yes, Mum," he laughed again. "Like geese."

"Well, son," she said, "I have to say good-bye now."

"Why?" he asked.

"Because I have to pack. It's time I go see your father and bring him back for your parole hearing next month."

"That's great. And Mom? Please don't say good-bye. It has such a final sound to it."

"Oh, no, it's not final at all. If you really understand the words, you'll use them easily when someone is about to take a journey."

"What do the words mean?" asked the son.

"Well, there is a story about the old English language that insists the word *good-bye* came from four words: "God be with ye." They just shortened it to the contraction *goodb'ye*."

"That makes sense," said her son.

He smiled as he hung up the phone. *Goodb'ye, Mom, and good luck!*

When the time came for the parole hearing, the young man felt calm inside his heart. All the teachings his mother had brought over the years had paid off, and he was now emotionally stable. His faith in God was deep, and his commitment to help young people strong. When the board members took their places, he was brought in to sit beside his parents.

"Good-bye!" said the other prisoners he had been in close contact with.

"Thanks!" he said as he walked down the long corridor with the sliding iron bar doors. "I'm a little nervous Dad," he said, sitting down beside his father.

His father took his shoulder and whispered something in his ear. The young man's face broke into a grin, and a light seemed to emanate from his whole being.

One of the parole officers called the meeting to order.

"First, we will hear from the victim's family," he said, giving the dead boy's parents a chance to speak.

They had lost their son so many years before, and all their grief seemed to have been saved for this moment.

"Well, I'm all for seeing him burn in hell!" said the dead boy's father.

The victim's mother sat quietly. When it was her time to speak, she was demure in her presentation.

"I am happy to be here," she said. "I have waited so many years to have this opportunity to speak with Isaac myself. My son Jesse has come to me in dreams many times over the years. Isaac, he asked me to tell you he has forgiven you, and I want you to know that I have forgiven you also."

The dead boy's father was outraged.

"What about my political stance if this scum walks free?" he ranted.

"Sir, you need to sit down," said one of the officials in charge.

"Sit down? You expect me to sit down?" he yelled, his hurt masked by anger.

"Yes, sir, or you will have to leave the room," said the officer, determined to have peace during the meeting.

The victim's mother began to cry.

"Um, sir." The young man in question stood up.

"What do you want?" The victim's father was beginning to soften his tone.

"First of all, I want to apologize for taking the life of your son. And second, I want you both to know that not one day has passed that I haven't thought about your boy and what a terrible thing I did."

The dead boy's father became quiet, and once again, the mother began to cry.

"Ma'am, I've made a huge mistake in life, but I want to go home now," he said. "I have been meditating for many years, and with the absence of the mind- and mood-altering substances I was taking, my violence has disappeared."

The victim's mother seemed to be coming back to life.

"I'm sorry," he said. "Really sorry."

The emotions in the room were thick, and the officials decided it was time to take a break. When the meeting reconvened, the father of the boy who had grown into a man was asked to speak.

"Well, folks," he began because he was a simple man. He had grown up in the country, and although he was extremely intelligent, he wasn't highly educated. "I don't know what to say, except I too had a big part to play in the death of your son. For so many years, I was a bad influence on my son's life, but now I'm working hard to change all that. If he's allowed to come home, you have my word that he will not see what he saw before going to prison. I was self-centered and did not support him in a way that was conducive to his well-being or connectedness in the community. His mother and I were divorced because of my poor attitude, and now I have the chance to set things straight."

When he sat down, the prisoner's mother stood up. She had tried to disguise her usual white clothing by wearing more conventional tones of tan and white. Her mala (prayer beads) was tucked inside her shirt, and the way she spoke was not her usual spiritual language. She thanked the parole officers for calling them together and said she'd been supporting the man in question for many years. She choked with tears as she looked over at the dead boy's mother.

"I'm sorry, too," she said. "For a long time, I didn't forgive myself for what happened to your son. I felt responsible because of the lifestyle I followed when my son was small. I too have worked hard to change my behavior over the years. Now I only hope and pray you can both find forgiveness in your hearts so you will not hurt so bad anymore."

The parole officers asked the young man to speak next. When he stood up, a great hush seemed to come over the room.

"I want to tell the truth, and I hope you will believe me when I say again that I'm sorry. My work will be going to help today's youth so maybe, just maybe, some other people won't have to hurt like you and my parents have. I just want to live my life as a free man. That's all I have to say."

When the parole hearing ended, there was great rejoicing all over the land. The mother got on the phone and let several people know that her son was coming home. His father was happy, and a tear even trickled down his face. They kissed their son good-bye, for his last day would be spent finishing up his affairs in prison and getting his belongings checked out. Before leaving, the woman moved close to her son.

"What did your father say that made you smile and light up when you first came before the parole board?" she asked.

He said, "I'm going to remarry your mother, and we're going to have a family again."

The mother smiled.

"Oh, he did, did he?"

They laughed like they had in the old days, and a big weight was lifted from the lives of many people.

CHAPTER 9

Together, We Can

THE WOMAN'S LIFE BEGAN TO change once she made up her mind to follow her heart. She had longed to be part of a family since childhood, but the karmas from her past had to be worked out. Her teacher gave her breathing exercises and a secret *sadhana*[3] that no one except his other devotees knew. She walked what she spoke until, one day, she had to leave the ashram. When she went to her teacher, he quickly agreed.

"It's your duty," he said, and he pointed to the door.

Her heart felt like it was breaking into 1,008 pieces as she left her guru's side, but like she had when she left her parent's home, she knew it was time.

"The guru is the highest," she wrote in her journal. "Please, God, no matter where my journey takes me or what other

---

[3] Sadhana: A Sanskrit word meaning "spiritual practice"

people I meet on the way, let me always remember his shining example as a human being, a mirror of your divine essence."

Blessed were her travels, and whenever she needed food or drink, the appropriate person or institution offered their obeisance. She felt loved, unlike the days before her sadhana, and the spiritual name her teacher gave her was known deep inside her being.

Although her real mother had died when she was just a baby, the woman decided to write her a letter. She believed in ritual and was glad when her uncle told her that her mother had also been psychic since childhood. He too had the gift, he told her, but many people his age were afraid of the truth so he'd kept the knowledge to himself.

"Never frighten people," he explained one morning at a family reunion. "If you think people are ready for the truth, then tell them what you see. Otherwise, keep it a secret and let them develop in their own way. They will reach out when they are ready to know. The doctor does not seek out his patients; the patients come to him."

"But what if I see them suffering?" the woman asked innocently, as she was not very bright in the ways of the world.

"If you see someone suffering, you must pray for their ability to reach out. But if you give the milk freely, no one will ever buy the cow!" he said, flashing a mischievous grin.

"Hey, my dad used to say that!" said the woman.

"Well, if one person calls you a horse, forget all about it, but if five people call you a horse, go buy a saddle!"

The woman suddenly had an idea. She put the letter to her mother in a small earthen pot. She knew the Indian tribes of North America used to send smoke signals in order to transmit messages to their dead ancestors. She put an offering of candy in the pot, along with some incense and a small cotton wick dipped in vegetable oil. When the wind picked up, she lit the cotton wick, watching the letter go up in flames.

"*Om Namo Bhagavate Vaasudevaya,*[4]" she chanted over and over, until all the ashes had blown away.

"There," she said, picking up the pot. "Now my mother has received my prayer."

Back inside the house, she passed a mirror in the hall. The photos of her mom that her father had given her as a young teen flashed through her mind.

I look a lot like my mother except for our clothes. I never used to dress very intelligently, the woman thought a little sadly. *I always wanted to be comfortable because I was such a mess inside. My clothing portrayed my inner landscape for sure! Well, now I'm going to step up to the plate and be all that I can be.*

She'd heard the term "step up to the plate" from a doctor of psychology on television. She had not liked his attitude the first time she saw him, but after a while she realized he really made a lot of sense. The letter to her mother was the most honest she had ever been. There always seemed to be a few hidden parts of herself that she would not reveal to anyone, as she was so afraid of rejection and unfair judgment.

I wonder where that comes from, she thought, washing the pot she had used for the ritual. *To wonder is to blunder, I know, but not in the case of self-reflection. In order to heal, I need to understand my negative patterns. I am going to write down every memory where I was afraid of rejection or judgment. Yes, that will certainly help.*

She picked up her pen and began to write. Before she knew it, she had worked through lunch, and it was time for supper.

Wow, I'm still not finished! she thought, and she kept writing.

---

[4] Hindu mantra for "surrender to God." *Vaasudeva* is another name for Krishna.

When her wrist began to hurt, she sat up, alarmed.

"It's me!" she said, right out loud. "It is me that judges and me that rejects!"

She thought of her high school years. A boy had phoned and she had not wanted to talk to him.

"I'm not home!" she had called out to her stepmother.

She was too afraid to tell him the truth; she didn't want to be his girlfriend. He didn't do anything wrong. He just wasn't the one for her.

Now what was so scary about that? Why couldn't I just tell the truth? Now I am still carrying that guy around like a sack of rotten potatoes.

The cats she had loved so long ago had been a disaster to kill. One day, her husband decided they would take a trip. She had always loved adventure, so when he asked what to do with the cats, she said, "I'll give them away!"

"Who's gonna want these ol' cats?" he asked. "Do you think you can find someone to take them by next week?"

The woman felt herself shrinking.

"We might as well take them out back and shoot them," he said. "They're only cats."

Turning her back, the woman felt sick to her stomach.

"Okay," she said, betraying her love for the two little creatures that looked up to her for food and nurturing.

As the woman busied herself packing for the trip, she happened to look out the bedroom window. There, on the mound of grass, was one of her cats. Blood gushed from one side of its head, and the saddest look was on its face.

"Oh, my God!" said the woman as she raced out to find her husband. "Look what happened!"

Tears were coming fast.

"Morrie has come back to haunt us!"

"Where?" he asked, looking where her finger pointed.

"The side of the house," she said. "Go get Morrie!"

When her husband came back, he tried to stay calm.

"Well, now I have to kill her. She is nearly dead. What else can I do but put her out of her misery?"

The woman closed her eyes like she had done much of her life when the pains of hers or other people's actions were beyond her repair.

"Okay, but do it quick," she said and went back inside the house.

The man put the cat in a blanket and took it out into the woods. When the woman heard the shot, part of her heart died with her kitten's love. The man's face looked ashen when he returned to the house. He did not know what else to do but wash the blood from his hands.

The next morning, the woman went outside to hang up the laundry.

"My God!" she exclaimed, and again she ran inside for her husband's comfort. "You are not going to believe what I just saw!"

"What?"

His wife's face looked like she'd seen a ghost.

"There in the field," said the woman. "Morrie is dragging herself back toward the house."

"No!" The man looked out the window.

"Yes," she said. "Now I'm really scared. We never should have tried to kill Morrie in the first place," she said, beginning to cry. "But it is too late! You must finish the job! Don't you realize she is suffering not only from the pain of the gunshot but because our love has been betrayed? She looked up to us almost the same as a child to a parent. When that love is betrayed, the child returns again and again, trying to make things right."

The woman picked a flower from a plant in the room.

"Offer this when you kill her. Tell Morrie we are sorry and that if she wants to come back again, she can take a human birth. This flower will go to the gods so they will know she is ready for human advancement. She never gave up but kept walking even when persecuted by those who loved her."

The man looked down at the flower. Its pink petals were lovely to smell.

"Well, if you say so," he said, and he walked out to do the terrible deed for the third time.

"Oh, and dear?" she said, because her maturity was now in place.

"Yes?" said the man.

"I love you," she said. "And that flower is also proof for God to know that we need forgiveness. You did not do the killing on your own. I gave the go-ahead, so I will help raise the child when it reincarnates.

"It's important that we get serious about life and stay together, *no matter what*. The lives of children are the most important because they make up the society of the next generation. If we do not stick together with the ideals of love and forbearance, the children's traditions will be lost and the race destroyed."

He looked rather strangely at the woman. Up until now he'd always thought her a bit touched, but the wisdom she was displaying seemed to make sense.

"Okay," he said, but this time he bent over to pick his own flower. "You know what?" he said rather quietly.

"What?" she replied, amazed at the glow flooding his body.

"Why don't you begin now? The cat wants your love, it's plain to see. I should have insisted all along, but I was intimidated by your funny ways."

"Funny ways?" asked the lady.

"Yeah, sure. You're always reading tarot cards and going to psychics for your future to be dissected before it even happens. You've scared the heck out of me many times by telling me things about myself that no one could have known but me."

"Those ways are not funny, but natural," she said. "We can all do the same if we get quiet inside. I just needed someone to congratulate me on my honors," she said rather shyly.

"Honors?" he asked. His look was blank.

"Yes. I never went very far in school," she admitted. "I was always more interested in the spirituality of the people than the worldly desires of fame and wealth."

"What do you mean you needed to be congratulated?" he asked. "Isn't that kind of egoistic?"

"Yes, but in a good sense. We will do a lot for appreciation that we would not do for money or fame. I needed someone to recognize my true worth as a spiritual seeker, and you just did."

She picked up the flower he had dropped when he bent over to pick up his own.

"We can walk together to help victims," she said. "In doing that, we will both be honored, not chastised, for all the harm we have caused in search of our own self-aggrandizement."

"Won't God want to punish us for hurting Morrie?" he asked.

"God *is* Morrie," she explained. "Look at the times Jesus told His disciples, 'Peter, you will betray me before the cock crows three times,' and 'Judas, you can handle the money.' Knowing their human frailties, God allowed them the suffering that would come from their transgressions. It's all about the lessons, and we just learned an important one."

Relieved, he said, "Yes, together!"

CHAPTER 10

Khelab

NOW THAT THE MAN WAS taking charge of his life, the woman was once again physically attracted to him.

What's this feeling? she asked herself with horror. *I thought I was all finished with that!*

She quickly went to her room to plead with God for some kind of understanding.

"I'm tired of physical attachment," she said, praising God for the years of reprieve from such impulses. "I don't want to go back to that, God," she whispered, hoping her husband would not hear. He had always been physically attractive to women even though his nose had been broken in fights and gaps made his teeth sit apart from one another. "I want to be free of all suffering and to raise my sexual energy up to be transmuted into spiritual energy. Please, Lord," she cried. "Please, help me to keep my focus on dharma.[5]"

---

[5] Dharma: Virtuous living or one's innate spiritual calling

The voice, which had been still for quite some time said, "We are making a child inside your womb. Stay abstinent from all penetration, and you will see the outcome blossom with a holy child."

"Oh, God!" she replied nervously. "My family already thinks I'm half crazy. Please don't push them over the edge in their belief that I'm a necromancer!"

"It has nothing to do with magic," the voice whispered in the quiet of her heart. "It is your dharma. You have always known it, and now is the time for its fulfillment."

"I am willing, but maybe I'm too old!" argued the woman.

"No, we planned the conception for a time when people knew you were way beyond your fertile years. We made certain it was a troubled woman of insecure birth that would lead the way so others would have hope that God is alive. We know the way of the world is doubt, rejection of purity, and the disaster of unrighteous living. When a capable source is at hand, we do our duty and use the vehicle for faith. Develop your relations with others. Keep to yourself about the pregnancy, and when you are in your seventh month, your friends will come to your financial and emotional aid."

"I don't know. I'm getting old," worried the woman. "Maybe the child would want a younger mother."

The voice was reassuring. "You are young. Be kind to your son, Isaac. He is used to being your baby even though he is now a man. Get him involved, and do not forget for one moment that you are being watched."

"I like that!" exclaimed the woman. "It used to make me paranoid thinking I was being watched, but not anymore. I know only loving and kind outcomes are the result of your guidance. Will you do me a favor?" asked the woman.

"What?" asked the voice.

"When my father reincarnates will you see to it that he has a mother and father who love and guide him all through his youth? There's no telling how long that will take, but hey! Who knows for any of us how long it will take?"

The voice didn't answer, but as the woman passed the mirror in the hall, she noticed a strange flash of light.

"I'm being watched!" she giggled. "I like having secret friends pulling for me."

As the days passed, she watched for signs of a baby, but nothing happened.

What's going on? I thought I was chosen to carry a blessed child in my womb.

A long time passed, but still, nothing happened. Then one afternoon, the sun was directly overhead. She thought she heard a rumble, and the sky clouded over. It began to rain, and she was sure she saw the moon emerge from behind one lone cloud. Before it disappeared, the thought, *Mother*, came to her, and she felt movement inside her womb.

Be careful, she told herself. *This must finally be my time. I will guide the child with all my knowledge, wisdom, and good vibrations. It will certainly be a girl!*

But directly following her thought of the child's gender came the prophetic announcement of its name.

Khelab is here!

As though floating in her mind, the letters took form as a name and then faded into a small heart.

"Buy me a tricycle and let Isaac teach me to wield it!" he commanded.

Wield it? Who uses language like that? she thought with a smile, patting her still flat belly.

"Isaac!" the child cried inside her womb. "I want Isaac!"

Well, Isaac is the only one I can turn to who will undoubtedly trust everything I say, the woman reflected. *After spending so many years confined in a lonely jail cell, he knows the interior of his mind better than any person I know, except my guru. If this child is a gift to him, then who am I to stand in the way?*

The mother was again aware of the thought transference from the child.

"I am not here *for* Isaac," he said. "I am here to walk *with* Isaac. We were once brothers, and now we will again be brothers. Only this time, he is ready to walk together. All competition is passed, and he now understands the dharma that will free many people. Dharma is righteousness. Dharma is a river that flows in the lives of virtuous people.

"When the spleen is in distress, the body can no longer eliminate what is not wanted. This puts the society of the body at risk. It is very much the same when the generation of children comes later in life. When people lose their vitality, the lessons gained are much harder to come by. This society of people will eventually see the outcome of their greed and nonreceptiveness to the ways of their ancestors."

"But *you* are coming to an older woman," said the lady with child.

"Yes, but this is a special gift, not your average birth. It will uplift the lives of many for eons to come. The manifestation of a holy birth is for the purpose of uplifting dharma. *Dharma* means 'correct living.' The man needs to support his wife and build a nest for their children. This is to be done in the spring of their lives, not the autumn when the leaves of their austerities are already falling to make compost for their next lives.

"Isaac and I have much work to do, and you and his father need to be jointly integrated into the teachings of the masters.

You are chosen due to your capability to love without condition. He was chosen due to his need to love without condition. Trust God; stay free from the poison of attachment, ego, and desire; and walk humbly forward doing your duty. All else will be provided in due course."

Wow, she thought when the child went quiet. *The quiet voice within is not so quiet anymore!*

"Very funny," said the voice, and she felt a strong bond to the child in her womb.

One day while hanging out the laundry, the woman saw a bright star in the eastern sky. It was so bright that when she went inside the house, she pulled open the curtains so she could watch it throughout the day.

What about the tendency for my blood to clot? I don't think it's healthy to be pregnant if my blood clots!

The boy's voice was becoming louder as the days passed. She could have a discussion with the little sage almost as though he were in the room.

"I *am* in the room!" Khelab exclaimed. "I am not in the body; the body is in me. My name means 'born to shine.' Like the bright star in the east, I was born to make people's lives bright by shining in the darkness to give them hope."

"And the blood clots?" she asked. "What should I do about that?"

"Well, the doctor will give you some chemicals, but they will deter your ability to contain the body I am forming."

"Should I go see the doctor?" asked the woman.

"No, do as you are doing. Stop and walk, stop and walk. Climb up and down the stairs, struggling to make the heart pump. Put a little castor oil in your tea and drink it right down. This will displace the ability of your blood to clot and guard you from further turmoil."

The woman shuddered. "Aren't there castor oil capsules? I heard it is horrible to taste!"

"Maybe, but remember, I come from an ancient time when these modern inventions were not in use yet."

"Okay, I'll do as you ask," said the woman, knowing there was no harm in trying.

She'd taken a pregnancy test just a year before when she thought she was pregnant. Because of her age, the people at the hospital looked like they thought they should get the straitjacket ready and unlock the doors to the padded cell she was about to enter.

"At least if they put you in a padded cell, I won't get hurt when I'm a toddler!" said the child.

"Very funny!" the woman laughed, feeling warm and happy inside her heart.

CHAPTER 11

An Attitude of Gratitude

ONE MORNING THE WEATHER TURNED cold, and the woman felt fear surrounding her. Nothing she did could sway the feeling, so she dropped to her knees and began to pray.

"Oh, Lord, I feel fear pervading my every thought," she said most respectfully. "The fiber of my existence is vibrating at a low degree, and I see pictures in my mind of terrified eyes. You are the love of all people. Won't you please let me know your truth, existence, and bliss?"

The Lord replied, "You are not the one afraid, but the receptor of great horrific acts being given up with an attitude of sorrow. The children born to child abuse are often receptors like this. Betray not your own mission, but surround yourself with an attitude of gratefulness. This will ensure that no harm can touch you."

By now the woman knew she could trust the still, quiet voice that came from her heart. She'd doubted for many years and then decided to trust and observe the results.

She got up from her knees and looked out to the backyard behind the house she was visiting. No home was hers, but every home had become hers. She looked in the mirror, but no flashes of light came shining from the reflective glass.

What would it be like to be the one who'd created many disastrous actions in their lives?

The woman didn't just mean taking a few candy bars from the local corner store but committing actual murder and other heinous crimes that signaled to society that a person was nothing more than an animal. She shuddered at the thought and then recalled the compassionate words of Jesus: "Do unto others as you would have them do unto you."

The woman went for a walk. For a long time, her youngest son had been in jail for a crime committed as a young teen. She thought about his behavior as a child, and then she thought about her own.

I never spoke out, she thought. *I never told anyone, least of all my parents, how I felt when they abandoned me for the people at the bar. I never told my mom how it felt that she died when I was a baby. And I never told my children how it feels when they blame me or their father for their own wrong choices. I did, however, say how it felt when they did something that made me feel happy. I must have blocked out those other feelings as a child, thinking other people were doing the same thing.*

When she'd gone to visit her son in prison, he had always held his shoulders up and tried to be jovial. Remembering a picture of herself as a little girl, she thought, *I often held my shoulders up as a child. Why was that?*

The voice that had helped her through many difficulties remained quiet. Just when she realized she was on her own, an image of her son appeared before her.

"Let me out of this prison, Ma," he begged. "I know it was you that put me here because I was bad. You're a witch, and everyone knows it."

She looked evenly at the vision of her son.

"What do people mean when they say I'm a witch?" she asked.

"They mean you cast spells and put powerful curses on people to make them do what you want. Most people, including Grandpa, my sister, brother, and many friends, are afraid of you."

"Maybe that's the fear I've been feeling, but, son?"

"Yes, Mom?" he said in the old, sweet voice she remembered from his childhood.

"I'm glad you're beginning to really talk to me. I can't control anyone, nor do I want to. I drew a circle at the beach one day and then stepped inside. After reciting some powerful words, I cried out to the ocean, 'Bring me a sweetheart!' and the circle began to resonate with sound."

"Did the sweetheart ever come?" asked her son.

"Oh, the sweetheart came all right, but not as I suspected. My heart had been bitter for many years, thinking the world had done me dirty."

"You sound funny when you talk like that," said the boy who was now a man.

"I'm part of all worlds but belong to none," I realized. "The attachment I used to feel for people has changed. Now I keep my focus on gratitude, and the end result is peace."

Just before her son's image began to fade, he said, "Mom?"

"Yes, son?"

"I'm always saying I'm sorry to you."

"Do you know why?"

"There you go again—analyzing my feelings."

"I'm not analyzing anything. I simply asked if you know why."

"Well, I'm not sure," he said, looking puzzled. "Do you know why?"

"Yes, but I'd rather not say. You'll figure it out yourself."

"Why won't you just tell me?"

"Because you lose a lot of respect for yourself when I give you all the answers. You need to bring forward your own inner guidance through prayer and self-reflection."

"Now that I'm asking, you won't tell me, and when I don't ask, you won't stop telling me!"

"You need to own your own problems, son. If you blame me, you'll be apologizing to me. If you don't blame me, you don't need to say you're sorry."

"I thought you weren't going to tell me!" he said.

His eyes sparkled, and a sweet grin spread across his face.

"Well, son," she said with a faint look of mischievousness, "you never could keep a secret."

"Now what the heck do you mean by that? That has absolutely nothing to do with what we were talking about!"

The woman whispered a sacred word in his ear. It was the one she used to keep evil out of her life. The young man grinned.

"I know that word already," he said. "You taught me that when I first began to study with you."

"Yes, but now it's time for you to begin to reflect on the word and its meaning. If you chant that name of God, you will certainly walk free from this prison you hate so much."

"How can that help?" the man wanted to know. "I said it for quite a while, and I'm still in prison."

"Did you reflect on the meaning?"

"That depends on what you mean by *reflect*. I know what the story is, and I know what the name means."

"Well, let me put it this way. When you were younger and rap music was in style …"

"In style?" he asked, laughing at his mom's choice of words.

"Yes, in style!" she said, laughing along with him.

He liked to hear his mom laugh. He mostly only saw her smile, and very few people could make her laugh so hard that her whole body shook from the inside out.

Clearing her throat like Miss Piggy from *The Muppet Show,* she continued. "As I was saying …"

He liked that too. She knew how to play even while giving him a lecture. She went on to describe the error many people make by listening to music, especially repetitive music, with the nature of sensual living.

She said, "Life is hard enough without someone singing, 'Kill, kill, kill those dirty bastards,' or 'Line 'em up, string 'em out, we're gonna party tonight!'"

"*Mom!*" he exclaimed. "I've *never* heard you talk like that!"

"Well, you don't hear me talk like that because I refuse to listen to those kinds of words."

"Sometimes, you hear those kinds of words from me," he said sheepishly.

"No, son. That's not what I hear from you. What I hear from you is that you saw some forgettable scenes in prison, and you are trying to give them to me because the pictures won't go away."

"Forgettable scenes that won't go away?"

"Yes, they're forgettable because they're not real, and they won't go away because you helplessly focus on them again and again. When people play music with headphones on or fall asleep in front of a TV, they are programming their minds like a programmer does a computer. They install the information and then, when the right keys are hit, bam! Out come the bad words, their fists, or the anger they keep locked up inside."

"You see it, huh?"

"Yes, I see it when you cut your eyes or make hissing sounds with your mouth. When the Dalai Lama speaks, he laughs so much that it's hard to hear his words. He is so full of joy that it bubbles right over like a frothy cup of root beer."

"Hey! What do you say we take a trip to Dairy Queen when I get out and have a root beer float? Would you drink one with me, Mom?"

"Well, today I might say no, but when you get out I might say yes. Why don't we make a pact?"

"What's that?" he asked with innocent-looking eyes.

"Why don't we say that, just for today, we'll keep our thoughts on living and enjoying life without the use of drugs? Just for today, we'll go to twelve-step meetings, seek our higher power, and do whatever it takes to gain control over our ability to keep the focus on ourselves. Just for today, we'll be unafraid. We'll hang out with people who are not using and find a new way to live. Think we could do that?"

"Yeah, but I'll feel like I'm a hypocrite because I'm not going to twelve-step meetings."

"When you were small, you didn't feel like a hypocrite when you pretended to play a guitar and ride a motorcycle!"

"No, but I was only a child then," he laughed. "That's a *lot* different."

"Well, now you're God's child."

"You're not going to twelve-step meetings."

"How do you know?"

"Because you said you don't belong there anymore since you wear white all the time."

"That's why keeping the focus on yourself will be so important. I went to kindergarten, and when I grew up I didn't need to go anymore, but still, I sent you."

"That's different, isn't it?"

"Yes, in a way, but not really. I still contact people who can help me if I'm in question about something. I stay clean from all drugs and alcohol no matter what, and I read the literature that most educates me at this phase of my development."

"What about the newcomer? Don't you think you should be there for the newcomer?"

"You might say I am," said the woman. "When you go to meetings, they'll hear a message of recovery from the depths of your heart. You'll know the fellowship's traditions, get a sponsor, and participate in service. When you hug someone of the opposite sex, you'll say, 'Keep coming back!' and word will get around that you're a powerful speaker.

"When you share at conventions, I'll be sitting at the back of the room. Without revealing my identity, you'll describe the years your mother tirelessly walked; hitchhiked; and took buses, trains, and airplanes to assist you through the throes of your addiction and out the other side.

"The women in the room will hear your story and be touched by the woman who never gave up on her son. Like Freddy Mata did with his mother, you'll ask your mom to come up to the front of the room and say a few words. The crowd will clap and cheer, and you won't even feel one pang of jealousy like I'm stealing your thunder. The recovering addicts in the room will hear a message of hope, and your heart will swell with pride because at last, you and your Ma will be on an even keel, and together you will help a lot of people."

"Mom?" asked the man.

"Yes, son?"

"Will you go out for coffee with us afterward?"

He grinned because he knew that the woman who always wore white didn't drink coffee.

"No," she said. "I'll respect that you need to be the star for a while."

"Mom?"

"Yeah?" she said in her old slang.

"I don't need to be the star anymore. God should be the focus, not me. If I give someone a fish, I feed them for a day, but if I teach someone to fish, I'll feed them for a lifetime."

"Wow," said the woman. "You really have changed. Well, I'll tell you what. If after the meeting your friends want to go out, maybe I'll take you up on that root beer float. But, son?"

"Yes, Ma?"

He knew when he called her *Ma* that she thought of the Divine Mother, which made her very happy.

"Will you do me a favor after we go out for the root beer float?"

"Yes, sure. Anything," her son promised.

"Don't tell your father. He doesn't think I drink!"

And they laughed and laughed, knowing that everything was going to finally turn out right.

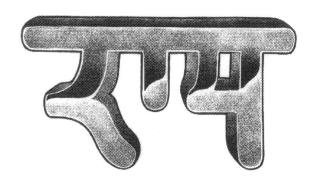

CHAPTER 12

Chant Ram! Ram! Ram!

"I HAD A VISION," THE woman's son told her one day as he sat down across from her in the prison visiting room. "The memory was as clear as a bell chiming in the church tower. I went to see my grandmother in Manitowaning, Ontario."

"You did?" the woman sounded surprised. Her son hadn't even been born when his family used to visit the old woman.

"Yeah, my dad was wearing a black cap. It was a little like a baseball cap with a brim in front, but it was flat on top, sort of like what a jockey would wear."

"Well, he was no baseball player, and certainly no jockey!" she said. "I don't know what that cap meant to him."

"Does everything have to mean something, Mom? I mean can't we just happen to be wearing a cap and it doesn't mean anything?"

"Actually, yes. If you are a little child and your mother puts a silly hat on you, then the hat has no significance. However, when you reach the age of discrimination and your faculties are working properly, everything means something."

"So in the vision," he continued, chuckling to himself—it used to upset him when his mother interjected her own thoughts when he was trying to tell her something—"I could see Dad with his mother, and you were in the background wearing a red shawl. I really liked that shawl. I thought you looked very sweet."

The mother said nothing.

"And then two small, white-haired kids ran up to you. They played with you for a while like little cherubs and then ran off to a big yard with scrubby but mowed green grass."

"That was clearly your grandmother's old place."

"Well, the one thing I couldn't understand was why you, Dad, and the kids were on one side of the fence and Dad's mom was on the other."

"There was no fence," said his mom, revisiting the yard in her memory.

"I'm sure there was a screened-in fence with silver bars," he said quizzically.

"That was the screen door," she laughed.

She remembered the day clearly. She'd gone with her husband into town to check the mail. When they returned, her mother-in-law wouldn't let her or her kids in the house. The elderly woman drank heavily, and she was certain that was the problem between her and her son, who had now grown into a man.

"What do you mean?" she had heard her husband say to the older woman standing behind the screen door that day. "I can come in but my wife can't?"

"Listen, son," said the old woman. "That is not your wife, and those two children do not belong to you."

He turned to look at the pretty woman who had always stood beside him. Her red shawl was draped gracefully over her shoulders, and her feet were bare because she said she could not breathe when she wore shoes. Although he didn't understand her funny ways, he never questioned them. Her undying love for him was sometimes more than he knew what to do with. No one had ever loved him like she did. So having his mother stand before him in judgment was like a brick wall behind the screen door of his worst nightmare.

"Mum, I'm coming in to talk to you," he told his mother firmly.

The woman with the red shawl went behind the house to play with her two blonde children.

They are the love of my life, she thought, watching them with great tenderness. All of a sudden, she felt a dark cloud lift, and everything seemed to stand perfectly still. The force of bliss emerged from deep within, and the karmic ties she had to the old woman in the house were suddenly made clear to her.

"The old woman was once very attached to you," said the voice she knew so well. "She loved you like her dearest friend, and then one day, you betrayed her with a kiss. You attempted to connect with her after that, but all was lost between you."

"Wow," said the modern-day mother's son. "That was weird. Did it really happen?" he asked.

"Oh, yes!" exclaimed the woman. "The voice went on to tell me that in a past life, the old woman's son had been her lover. When I came along, he was so charmed by my grace and beauty that he left her and married me. When the karmic bonds were broken that day, the old woman saw the reality of who I was standing next to her so-called son, and the rage of the past welled up inside her."

"What did you do?" asked the man who was now the present-day woman's son.

"Well, I always had a great deal of faith in the voice that spoke to me from beyond the veil."

"Beyond the veil?" he asked.

"Yes, the veil between superficial reality and reality. It is as real as the red shawl I wore that day."

"Where did you get that shawl?"

"Oh, that's not so important," she said. "The main lesson I had to learn was to see the old woman's pain and not hate her."

"Did you hate her?"

"No, I actually loved her. She had a drinking problem. Every time she felt her rage coming up she would drink alcohol to medicate herself so she would not feel."

"What can people do with the rage they have stored up in their hearts?"

"People don't store rage in their hearts," said the woman. "All rage is stored in the body and the mind. That rage, if not purified, will worm away at the person until, eventually, sickness or death comes to visit and finish the job."

"So what could the old woman do?"

"She could not do anything, but I could. In order to free myself from her curse, I had to love her with my whole heart. I could see she was hurting, so I simply waited for your father to come back outside and tell me what to do."

The younger woman seemed to distance herself for a few minutes and then had an idea.

"When you go back to your cell today, relax and enter into the vision you had. Imagine yourself burying a banana in the backyard of your grandmother's house. The banana signifies all things beautiful and clean."

"Mom, I'm not my brother. I don't really do those weird things you tell me."

"I know, son, but this time you must keep your focus on yourself. You came to the woman wearing the red shawl in the yard that day. You are supreme consciousness embodied in the physical and mental child that came to help that woman, who of course is now me. If all this sounds too weird …"

"Boy, does it!" said the man.

"Please do not interrupt! This is serious. Listen to what I am telling you. The voice told me that when you grew up …"

"Hey, wait a minute! I wasn't even conceived yet!"

"Well, what does *conceived* mean?" asked the woman.

"You know, to have a baby."

"No. Many people erroneously think they can physically make a baby, but the sperm and egg coming together is not the full plan. The conscious effort must be there."

"What about victims of rape?"

"Victims of rape are operating under the laws of transgression. A divine birth is different."

"What do you mean *a divine birth*?"

The woman smiled.

"Listen, son. Sri Krishna had a vision one day that he encompassed everything. Jesus knew from birth the mission he had to complete, and Rama[6] denied it when people told him he was the embodiment of God."

"What does this have to do with me?"

"The fact that you had that clear vision of your dad in the black cap, me in the red shawl, and your siblings running near me in the yard verifies what I always knew; you heard

---

[6] Rama: A Hindu god

my prayer. You came to help mankind from just the kind of suffering that woman endured."

"Please forgive me, Mum," he said, using his childhood name for his mom. "But I can't cope with all this hocus pocus."

The woman looked dismayed.

"I thought you were ready to know the Truth."

The young man saw a light forming in her forehead just above her eyebrows. The light seemed to get larger and larger until the whole room emanated from the radiance.

"Mum?"

"Yes?" she replied, the twinkle in her eyes as bright as four-carat diamonds.

"I see some of the things you say, but it frightens me."

"I know, son. Chant 'Ram, Ram, Ram,' and all the fear will disappear. Ram was the warrior who brought the light into the darkness. He was the embodiment of compassion and love who fought for dharma. If you will chant his name, his love will awaken the Truth in you."

"I love you, Mom."

"I love you too, sweetheart," she said.

"Am I the sweetheart you received that day at the beach when you said those magic words?"

"Yes, I thought I wanted a man to love, but what I really wanted was for my son to come home. Our family was, and is, blessed by your presence. You may appear to be the youngest, but in all reality you are the eternal Lord of the Immortals, the Great Amarnathji Maharaj."

He smiled when she touched his feet with reverence.

"Mom, I feel weird when you do that."

"I know, son. Don't take it too hard when I say I'm not your real mom."

"What?" he said.

"Just kiddin'," she said, bringing him back to the earth plane he loved so much.

"When you said that, I felt a jolt!"

"I know, son. It's my duty to usher you among the three worlds."

"Three?" he asked.

"Yes. You, me, and the divine. Trust me, son. I know the Truth."

He laughed. "You are the only one who could get away with this!"

"I know. That's because I'm your *ma*!"

And they linked arms and laughed like they had done so many times in the past.

CHAPTER 13

Think Only of Peace

THE WOMAN CONTEMPLATED HER JOURNEY with much care before leaving to see her ex-husband. The time of year was spring, and the blossoms were still in their seed form.

The tree of life is very strange, the pensive lady thought. *While we look outwardly to the world, there is another place inside that is the exact reflection.*

She'd always been the quiet type, except for the days she'd been exploited by the wrong thinking of her family, friends, and teachers at school. Thought waves penetrate even steel, she now knew, but back then her intellect had been as pure as a child's, reflecting the images of her environment.

After growing up in an atmosphere of neglect, she wanted to help others who were living in that same shameful experience. The woman knew that in order to influence the minds of those around her, they too had to become pure so they could absorb the teachings being passed down through the enlightened masters of spirituality.

Why don't people understand? It's plain to see that two plus two equals four. If you drink more than one beer, you will inevitably get drunk. If you get drunk, you will say things you don't want to and permit others to have their way with your body and mind in an attitude of deceptiveness.

As the woman packed her suitcase, she thought about the bicycle her ex-husband had given her for Easter one year. He'd left her special surprise in the kitchen that morning after the two of them had decided to give their relationship another try.

I know what was wrong. I tried to keep him to myself, and he loved people. He liked to please them and serve them in his charming way. This time I'll make sure he has that opportunity. I'm tired of living selfishly, thought the woman, but the quiet voice was kind.

"You weren't being selfish," it explained. "When you got back together with your ex-husband after your divorce, he did not commit to the relationship. You needed time alone to secure your romance, and then you could have walked together as one."

Will it be the same this time? she wondered, and again, the quiet voice interjected its healing force.

"No, this time things will not be the same, because the mission has changed. You were trying to get his forgiveness, thinking it was you who caused all the errors in your relationship. Now you've grown, and you realize that each individual is responsible for his own actions. We all have the integral force of love and discrimination planted deep within. It is our duty to play the game of life in a way that is conducive to the well-being of all creatures."

"But don't we influence one another?" asked the woman, beginning to doubt that the voice could be the Absolute, the One without a second.

"Yes, we influence others, but that influence comes through choice. God gives us the final say. Admit it. If you really don't want to do something, you won't. The conviction must be spiritual, however, or it can be based in revenge or resentment. We cannot pretend to be pure any more than a clear glass of water held up to a microscope can hide its impurities. We can, however, strive to do our best just one day at a time, and that striving sometimes means acting *as if.*"

The day finally came for the woman to leave her domain of many months. She'd received the message that her ex-husband had recently sent through her son. The boy didn't know all of his father's cunning ways, but she did. The art of sending a message through an innocent bystander came from the Native Americans. They knew that the propensity of most people is to talk about what they have heard. If something was to be kept secret, the worst thing you could say to an unsuspecting mind was, *Don't tell!*

The clothes she packed were simple. The satchel she carried did not hold much, as she knew her feet would often be her only means of transportation. She thought about her dad traveling around the world by himself with only a small shoulder bag.

What will my ex-husband say? she wondered again and again, until finally, she put the thought right out of her mind.

Her youngest son, the boy who had lost his early life to the throes of addiction, had cried out with tears in his eyes one Christmas morning.

"You broke it!"

She'd shaken the package he had wrapped with his own hands, and the tinkle of broken glass was a sure sign that her curiosity was not conducive to bringing a good outcome! Seeing his distress, she had vowed to let her gifts be revealed in their own time. Over the years, the woman had kept her promise, but she thought of her psychic ability as different. She'd continued to look into the future and the past to resolve the problems of her present moment.

Well, that is silly, she thought as she purchased her bus ticket. *The present moment is really all we have! Anything could change in this impermanent world, and because of time and space, the psychic realm too has its limitations. I think I'll do as my teacher explained and keep my focus on peace. If I concentrate only on peace, then the outcome must be the same.*

The bus driver was smoking a cigarette just outside the open doors as she went to climb the stairs.

"Excuse me, will you please smoke somewhere else so we don't have to breathe the toxins coming from your smoke?" she asked easily.

"Certainly!" said the driver, moving away from the door.

Peace, thought the woman. *Think only of peace.*

A baby began to cry.

"Would you like to change seats with me?" asked the woman. "If you sit near the front of the bus, the baby won't be so frightened. All the strange faces crowded around him are certainly scaring him."

"Well, thanks," said the baby's mother. "I wanted to sit up front but thought maybe I should sit closer to the toilet at the rear of the bus."

"Babies are sensitive and smell things we can't," said the woman, focusing on peace. "They sense with their fine, soft skin, and some noises are extremely loud. If you would like to have my seat, I will check back with you to see if you need anything from the restroom during our journey."

The baby began to smile with the windows at the front of the bus surrounding him. The bus driver turned on some music. The old woman sitting next to the peaceful woman began shifting in her seat.

"Are you okay?" asked the lady in white.

"No," said the old woman. "That radio interferes with my hearing aids. The little screeches give me a headache."

"Why don't you try turning them off?" the kind woman asked. "My uncle does it whenever he goes into a crowded place. No one will be talking to you for a while, and just think! You will be exempt from listening to the loud noise of the bus engine, the traffic when the driver opens the door, and all the different cell phone conversations!"

"Well, that is a wonderful idea! By the way, how did you get to be so smart?" asked the old woman.

"I travel quite a bit to visit my son. He has been in prison for many years."

"Oh, I'm sorry," said the old woman.

"Why are you sorry?" asked the younger of the two.

"Well, that must be awful hard having to see your son in the place where criminals have their way."

"Yes, in that way, it has been excruciatingly painful. But I realized after a while that if I did what my spiritual teacher taught me, the pain would go away."

"Do you mind if I ask what that was?" asked the old woman.

There were deep creases embedded in her face from years of worry. Her swollen ankles had most likely come from chasing broken dreams, and the hearing aids were a reminder that she had not listened when her inner self had prodded her to go right instead of left.

"He said, 'Focus only on peace, and do not worry about a thing. Whatever you focus on will be what appears in your life.'"

The old woman looked excited.

"Well, no wonder! All this time I wanted to help my husband of many years to stop drinking. Over and over, I would nag and plead with him to please, put that booze away and stop drinking! My children, all nine of them, failed in school. I wanted them to do well in life so I kept saying, 'Don't be losers! Losers never advance in life! Losers never make enough money! Losers don't concern themselves with anyone but only think of their own selfish desires!'

"My neighbors had a dog. That dog barked like a crazy hound all the time. I would yell, 'Stop barking! Stop it! Stop barking!' All during the day and throughout the night, I would open my window to scream at that dog."

A light seemed to glow around the old woman's face.

"Hmmm, peace, eh?"

"Yes, focus only on peace. What appears outwardly is what emanates from within."

"Well, do you think I can make my husband stop drinking?"

"*Think peace!*"

"And what about my kids? Do you think they will ever change?"

"Think only of peace!" the woman guided.

The long ride had been fruitful. As the bus pulled up to her stop, the younger woman swung her backpack onto her shoulders and waved good-bye. As she walked toward her daughter's home, she heard the old woman call out through the bus window.

"Think peace!"

Her smile was big, and a bright halo shone clearly around her head.

Whew, what a trip! the lady thought with a smile. *Peace, peace, peace. What else could possibly be sought by any intelligent creature? Even animals seek out the peace and quiet of nature.*

Hmmm, I wonder if my daughter likes to go out in the canoe. I would like to take the whole family for a ride, but I need a good navigator. Peace, only peace.

The next day as she unpacked the gifts she'd brought for her family, the woman realized she did know someone who knew how to drive a canoe. She could hear the voice of her youngest son.

"*Drive* a canoe? You're silly!"

She smiled.

What a good time they'd had at their three-day trailer visits in the prison. Peace. Think only of peace.

Someone was knocking on the door. When she went downstairs, there was a note from her daughter on the kitchen table.

"Mum, I'll be right back. I've gone to get some groceries."

I had better answer the door, thought the woman. *It might be one of my daughter's friends. Peace, only peace.*

The person standing at the door took her by surprise. He was holding a red rose and wanted to know if she still liked canoes.

"Yes," she replied rather shyly, but she admitted that the only way she would go was if the whole family could be part of the adventure. Her ex-husband smiled.

"I thought you might say something like that," he said, pointing to his van. "I brought life jackets for the children. The three adults can swim if anyone falls in."

"Well, that's no good," said the woman. *Peace, think only of peace.*

"Yes, it'll be fine," said the man with a firm sound to his voice. "I'm a good swimmer, and besides, I'm sure the canoe won't tip over."

"No," said the woman. "On an airplane they teach people to put on their own oxygen masks before helping their children. We will get enough life jackets for everyone."

Peace, only peace, she whispered to herself.

"That's what I thought you might say," said the man. "You always were stubborn when it came to getting your own way."

"Aren't you glad?" asked the woman as she linked her arm through his.

By the time they got everything ready, it was late afternoon. As the boat left the shore, the water was crystal clear. The rippling wake behind the canoe scattered the sun's reflection into a million sparkling diamonds.

"Look over there!" said the father of the girl with three kids.

"Dad, you won't believe this, but I still remember a canoe ride we took when I was small. You did exactly the same thing even then. You pointed at some ducks and a beaver swimming on its back. You wanted Mom for your wife," she said with a grin, being the instigator she loved to be.

"Yeah, you're right about that," said the man as he paddled along.

Peace, peace, peace, the woman chanted in her mind like a mantra.

"We will be at the shore soon. Who's ready to eat?" she asked in her grandmother voice.

She liked the role of grandmother, and for as long as she could remember, she had the image of family permanently tucked in her heart. Now here she was, finally getting to play the role she had dearly hoped for as a young girl.

"I loved my grandmother," the woman spontaneously said, interjecting her thoughts.

Just then, she caught a glint from her daughter's right hand.

"What was that?" she asked the girl from the next generation.

"Your grandmother's ring," she said. "For a long time I kept it locked in the jewelry box because it brought me so much sadness."

"Sadness?" asked the woman who was now the grandmother.

"Yes, sadness. Whenever I put the ring on, I thought of you. I've missed you a lot, Mom," she said with tears forming in her eyes.

"I know, hon'," replied her mother.

She liked to call her daughter *hon'* because it gave her the message that she was sweet but, more important, that she was loved in a familiar way.

"I'm going to wear it from now on," said the woman's daughter.

"Thanks, babe," she said. "To you I gave the ring, but more important, I passed along my vow to help people find peace."

"What do you mean?" asked the beautiful young mother.

"When I was a child, a teacher took me to the cinema. He bought popcorn and sodas, but all I could do was look at those poor people in the movie who were suffering from the toxic environment they lived in."

"It helped me a lot when you said I should stop smoking," said the woman's daughter. "And remember the time you phoned the police on my husband?" she asked.

"Yes, I am listening," said her mom.

"Well, I never thought I would live to see the day he would forgive you for that!"

"Forgive me?"

"Yes, that really tore our family apart."

"Honey, peace does not tear anything apart."

"What does that mean?" she said with a bit of an edge. "I'm not talking about peace. I'm talking about the night you phoned the police on my boyfriend."

"Do you think you are married?" asked the mother, trying to make her point.

Most people thought she just wanted to be right, but the truth was, she just wanted peace. Her daughter looked quizzically at her dad.

"You love your dad, don't you, honey?" said the mom.

"Yep, I love my dad."

The young woman tended to use sarcasm whenever she felt attacked.

"I'm making a point," said her mom.

"You usually do." Her daughter rolled her eyes.

Peace. Think peace, she whispered inside her head.

The father was watching. He thought his daughter could be rude and disorderly most of the time. Her attitude toward him was that of an angry mother toward her unruly child. He did not like being disrespected this way, but so many years had passed, and he did not know how to stop the vicious cycle.

"Terra?" said her mom.

"What?" she answered.

Her father and the three children were watching as the young woman looked defiantly at her mother.

"I love you," said the older woman.

"Then why did you leave?" asked the little girl.

Her voice had shrunk back to a long time ago. She seemed to be behind a thick wall, and her mother was taking it down one brick at a time.

"Terra," said her mom again.

"What?" the girl answered with extreme rudeness.

"You are my favorite daughter, honey."

"Yeah, right," she said. "What about all those women you sponsor?"

She knew her mother had a weakness for *losers*!

"Those women are so dear to me, but not one could ever replace the love I hold in my heart for you."

"And why do you have to spoil things by saying I am your favorite?" she said. "That makes me feel better than others or not good enough!"

"Well, honey—"

"Don't call me honey! My name is Terra. T-E-R-R-A!"

The kids were watching with their mouths wide open.

"I know your name, Terra," said her mom. "I named you, remember? I loved you from the first time I knew I was pregnant with you until this very moment."

Peace, peace, peace. Think only of peace, the woman chanted quietly, again and again.

"Well, I don't know why you gave me such a stupid name," said the now belligerent girl. "Why couldn't you just pick a normal one so I could at least find a cup with my name on it?"

At this, everyone began to laugh.

"Your name on a cup?" asked the woman.

"You may all think that is funny, but as a child I wanted to find my name somewhere—on a bag, a cup, even a magnet, but no! Nothing had *Terra*, only *Tara*. Mum, all your life you've had to be different. Like sending me to school to make tortillas for show-and-tell. Do you know how stupid I felt?"

"Tell me more," her mother said, knowing her daughter needed to vent the anger she had kept pent up inside for so many years.

She was finally strong enough to see it for what it was—the past. The young woman said a few more things to her mom, and then all of a sudden a loon stood up and danced across the water.

"And you know what, Mum?" she said.

"What?" replied her mom.

"No offense to you or Dad, but I remember the day my real dad left."

"You do?" asked the mother.

"Sure," said the girl. "I was playing with Josh in a room full of beds when my dad came in and picked me up. He held me real tight and said, 'I love you, Terra. You will always be my daughter, no matter who raises you.'"

"I'm sorry about all that, Terra," soothed her mom.

"It's okay," said the young woman, and then she started to cry.

It was as though all the years of mistrust, hatred, defensiveness, and sorrow had broken through, and the young woman cried and cried. The older woman, now a grandmother, motioned to everyone not to touch the girl but to let her have a minute to cry. When she gave a nod, everyone put their hands on Terra. They said they loved her, and the father let the boat drift off its course. The canoe caught up in some reeds, and everyone agreed it was a good time to have their picnic. While the father started a fire, the mother and daughter walked on the rocky shore.

"You know what, Mum?" she asked.

"What?" her mom answered, knowing how vulnerable her daughter must be feeling.

"I love you."

"I love you too," said the woman, feeling her age.

Over the years, there had been many difficulties in their family, but now she knew those obstacles were stepping stones to peace.

"Why don't we move to BC together?" asked the girl's mother.

"Yeah," said the girl. "We could do that."

"What is holding you back, Terra?" her mom questioned, trying to use the girl's name.

"You can call me hon'," she said. "I was just being a bitch, as usual."

"You really hated it when your dad used to hold you under the chin and call you a bitch didn't you?"

"No, I really hated it when you didn't stop him from saying I'm a bitch."

"Terra?"

"What?"

The daughter's defiance was now gone, and she seemed weak, almost like she was extremely tired.

"I am really sorry for how I acted," said her mom.

"Me too," said the girl.

"What do you mean?"

"A lot of times I was just trying to get a response from you. Dad couldn't stand rude children, and I knew how much you loved children. I figured if I was bitchy, I'd get a reaction from him. Then you'd come to my rescue and we could go back to my real father, but it never worked."

"Do you want to find your dad … your real dad now?"

"My real dad is right over there," she said with a weak smile. "Isaac is my brother, and that is *our* father. The land we grew up on should go to all three of us kids, not just Isaac," she said.

"Well, honey, people are funny with their own blood. When my dad left my stepmother and her children …"

"You never considered them as your real family, Mom."

"I know, but somewhere deep inside I knew my stepsisters, Liz and Susan, loved my dad. Well, Liz did, for sure. Susan wanted to, but he saw her as the depiction of the fat, lazy stepdaughter who made his own precious daughter work hard to make up for her lack of ambition."

"Did you see Susan as fat and lazy?"

"It is true she was overweight and sickly, but not through any fault of her own. She needed a loving father to make her feel wanted. She had a hard time with men because her mother never found contentment with the man she was with."

"If I leave my husband, will my children hate men also?"

"They may hate you, but you know what, hon'?"

The mother and daughter were now back to normal speaking.

"What?"

"The truth is your husband needs to get on board with what is right. He needs to realize what a beautiful woman he has right now and get down on his knee to ask for your hand in marriage."

"I don't believe in marriage," said the girl who was emerging back into a woman.

"A few minutes ago you said, 'If I leave my *husband,* will my children hate men?'"

"Yeah, I guess I did," said the girl.

"Do you want peace in your heart, Terra?" asked her mom.

"It sounds good, but I have no idea what that means."

"Well, peace is not something that can be explained; it must be experienced."

"What can I do?" asked the girl.

"You can begin saying to yourself, 'Think peace! Think peace! Think peace!'"

"I can try, but I'm used to saying, 'I'm a bitch! I'm a bitch! I'm a bitch!'"

"You're no bitch," said her mom.

"Yeah, my dad was right. I'm a bitch."

"Well, that way of thinking will not bring peace, so if you don't want the same kind of life you have had so far, you have a choice. You can inwardly chant 'I am a bitch,' and outwardly, chaos will reign. If you inwardly chant 'Peace, peace, peace,' then outwardly peace will reign. As you think, so you shall become."

"So does that mean I'll be a hippie and wear bell bottom pants like you used to?" she asked with a smile.

"Yes, that is exactly what I mean!" laughed her mom.

She was glad to have her daughter back. She had missed her loving ways and never knew the things she said that day had been bothering her all those years. The husband-to-be of the woman of peace suddenly let out a whistle.

"Do you think Dad loves me, Mum?" she wanted to know.

"Baby, Dad loves you so much. It doesn't mean he doesn't love Isaac or Josh. Love does not diminish itself, but expands. The more we love, the more we *can* love."

"I love you, Mum," said the daughter.

"I'm hungry!" said her mom. "What do you say we go eat?"

"Mom?"

"Yes, honey?"

"I'm not too interested in eating chips or drinking sodas anymore."

"Me either. I only want peace, and those things do not bring peace."

The woman thought about how much she loved her children, grandchildren, and the man she had never stopped calling husband. When they got to the campsite, the kids yelled, "Surprise!"

The grill was filled with veggie burgers, and her ex-husband poured fruit juice into enough cups for everyone to have a drink. The kids were happy when their grandpa gave them chips because they knew nothing about peace. They liked the salt and the crackle as they bit into the thin, delicate morsels.

"Well Ter', may peace be with us all!" said her mom.

The young woman laughed and held up two fingers in the shape of a V.

"Yeah," she sighed, as though a long journey was about to begin. "Peace," she said.

The father looked suspiciously at the two women.

What have they been up to? he wondered, but then he laughed.

"Oh, what the heck? Peace!" he called as he flipped the veggie burgers onto whole-wheat buns.

"Peace!" yelled the children, and everyone laughed and poked at the fire with big smiles on their faces.

CHAPTER 14

Shine

Now that Khelab was there for Isaac to play with, Isaac felt like he had a purpose in life. They spent hours together; "wielding" the tricycle was just one of the activities the elder brother taught.

"Now, son, you must take the boy to be baptized," said his mother.

"Was I baptized?" asked the man, always to be known as a boy to his mom.

"Well, no," she said.

"Then Khelab will not be either."

"Then why don't you both go?"

"Was Joshua baptized?"

"No, but I was so young and rebellious when I had him."

"And Terra? Was she baptized?"

"Um, no. None of you were."

"Mom, I think the worst thing you can do is to set Khelab apart from the rest of the family. He is one of us, so let him be one of us. If he is a god come to save the world from sin, then I'm sure he won't want to be separated from us in any way, shape, or form."

"You always were my saving grace, son."

"No, Ma. I'm just a boy in your eyes and a god in mine. That is why I can't make any real progress. If I'm to succeed in this world, I must make every effort to take my place amongst men and women, not above them. Remember, together we can."

"Son?" she asked demurely. "Do I act that way? I mean, do I act like I think I am better than other people?"

"Yeah," he said. "You do it a lot, but I love you, so it doesn't matter to me."

I wonder why I started doing that? she thought as she walked to the sink to start the morning dishes. *I liked the story of Mary, and Jesus was hung way up high above the people. Maybe that is what happened.*

The still voice inside the woman had been quiet for some time.

When I am on the right track, it is quiet, but when something needs fixing or danger is about to come, it is right there for me. Why is it so quiet now? I really need fixing if I think I am better than other people!

"You don't," she heard.

"What?" she asked, right out loud.

The voice was unexpected.

"You don't think you're better than anyone."

"Oh, I have!" said the woman.

"Exactly. You have in the past, but you have already changed. *Let the past go.*" And the voice went back to its source.

Hmmm … let the past go. That is not easy!

At their first meeting, her spiritual teacher had told her, "Keep your focus on the divine, and you need never fall back again."

She thought she could never live up to such a tall order! But right from the start, she obeyed every word of his direction. For many years, she had filled her head with the Yoga Sutras of Patanjali and studied the teachings of India's spiritual masters. She constantly listened to and sang songs of God's glory and took heed only of the wisest of his devotees.

They are all a form of God, she thought at first, but then she recalled the teachings she knew to be true.

"If you look at the road through a muddy windshield, you're bound to cross the line and get into trouble. God is truly inside each and every vehicle we call the body, but know for sure that some are too dangerous to be put on the road with other traffic."

That must be like criminals, she realized. *No one can live safely if they are not cleaned up and put on the right track. Well, I am going to help make that happen!* she thought with determination.

"You are already making that happen!" said the voice. "Look at your two sons. They are making great headway because you helped them to help themselves. You did well for a while with your brother and sister-in-law, but then you got afraid. 'What if they see me for who I truly am?' you worried."

"Well, who *am* I?" asked the woman.

"I am the One, second to none," replied the voice.

"Yes, but who am *I*?" asked the woman again.

Nothing. Just quiet. She looked around the room. She remembered her teacher's saying, "Looking for God outside is like searching for your son who is sitting on your shoulders. If you have a hundred-dollar bill in your pocket but forget it is there, you think you are broke. The money was there all along; you just forgot you had it."

Now the woman felt shy.

I am too afraid to think of myself as God. I may become egotistical or full of wrong ideas about what that means.

"Just shine," she heard the voice say.

"Just shine?"

"Yes, and the rest will happen by itself."

The Shining was a movie she hadn't liked very much. It was written by a man who loved to scare people.

"No," the voice assured her. "He had a good imagination, it's true, but most of the time, he just wrote about the ways of the world. You could never stand hearing the truth because you felt like it was your responsibility to change everyone and everything."

"Why?" asked the woman, nearly in tears.

"If I give you a bushel of apples and three are rotten, what is the first thing you're going to do?"

"Say thanks for the rest that are ripe and ready to eat."

"Good. Now, be honest—what will you do?"

"Take out the three rotten ones."

"Correct. And what will you do with the three rotten ones?"

"Give them to someone I do not like!"

She was playing with the voice, but like a strict schoolteacher, the voice was not playing back.

"I am going to throw the apples on the compost heap," she said. "Then I'll wash the slime off the good ones so they don't rot."

"Exactly. Now what do you think will happen when you go around helping victims of criminal activities?"

"I don't get the correlation," admitted the woman, now paying close attention.

"Well, the criminal, of course, is the rotten apple, but who is the victim in this picture?"

"The bucket?"

"Yes! Not the other apples, because the other apples are whole, juicy, ripe fruits ready to be eaten. The victim separates from the whole out of fear. The victim becomes the container, identifying completely with the mind/body complex."

"So how do I fit into this picture?" asked the puzzled woman.

"Well, look at it this way," said the all-knowing, ever-present voice. "If indeed I am God, then there is nothing to fear because the 'I AM' is right inside of you."

"Yes, but isn't it inside of everyone?"

"Yes! That's the point we are trying to make here. If we love one another and point to the truth, then no victim can remain because there will be no identification with the barrel that holds the good and bad apples."

"What happens to the bucket of apples?" she honestly wanted to know.

"The world continues on and on, but the identification process changes. I am husband; I am wife; I am daughter; I am son—all of these manifestations are equal because of the common denominator I am."

Whew, I will never be able to explain that to people! thought the woman.

When the dishes were done, she swept the floor.

I am the sweeper. I am the saint. I am the mother. I am the son. Wherever the "I am" comes into focus is the connection between people.

"Does the lion go around saying, 'I am the lion?'" asked the lady, sweeping the carpet inside the door.

"No, animals are instinctual," the voice answered. "They do not have the subtle energy centers or power vortexes called chakras, like the highly developed human being."

"Well, how can they evolve from plain animals to more-developed human beings?"

"They prove themselves at whatever level they're at. The proof is the strength that lifts us from one level to the next."

"Is that why we prove math problems on the side of our page?"

"No, that is just an exercise to ensure the student did not copy. Young people are filled with the desire to create. Making practical jokes and not doing their homework are normal for their age group. 'Do your homework, class,' the teacher will say. But most students would rather run outside and play or sit beneath the stars at night, listening to raccoons washing their food."

The woman felt kind of tired. *Peace, only peace. This is all too much for my weary brain.* And then she realized something. *I am young; I am old; I am woman; I am man. All these are temporary, but the "I AM" is constant.*

Wherever there was life, she could see the glory of God. The ones who had realized themselves were few and far between. Why, only yesterday she had walked through the mall. There in the store windows were female mannequins dressed in skimpy outfits. The nipples of their breasts were made to show, and the message was none other than "I am this body!" One even had her nipples painted like little stars right on the outside of the garment. The female mannequin appeared very happy to be a product of this odd display of her sexuality.

Can you imagine? Baby girls do not have a chance growing up in a society with images of this sort staring them in the face!

She spontaneously reached into her pocket and pulled out her prayer beads.

Om shanti,[7] *shanti, shanti,* she chanted silently.

---

[7]   Shanti: Peace

Touching each bead, she quickly moved the mala that was draped between her middle finger and the thumb of her right hand. The ring and pinky fingers lay behind as a support.

Om, shanti, she finished at the 109th bead.

The last bead was called the guru bead. It was separated from the others, but she didn't know why.

I'll ask my teacher at the next retreat, she thought, and then she got very still.

I don't like him anymore, she said to herself. *He really hurts my feelings sometimes.*

"What does he do?" came the voice, sounding very compassionate.

"Well, he never asked how I was when I returned from the hospital. He doesn't say, 'How is your son?' any more when I come to visit, and always, always, he excludes me from being one of his teaching disciples."

"Did you ever tell him this?" asked the voice.

"Are you kidding?"

"Actually, no," the voice said, remaining neutral. "If you have a problem, you should go directly to the source."

"That's pretty hard to do, but I guess until I tell the truth, I will never know the outcome."

"Exactly," said her conscience.

My conscience? thought the woman.

"Yes," said the voice. "Everyone was given a conscience."

"What is the source of that wisdom?" she asked.

The voice guided, "Go deep inside and find out. Where do the rivers come from but the ocean? The rain is the moisture absorbed into the clouds, and every morsel of food we eat is from the divine. It all has 'Ram' printed at the heart."

"Even potato chips?" asked the lady, still trying to joke with the voice.

"If the potato is covered in deep fried fat, then the results of the 'Ram' will be clouded over also."

"You mean we become what we eat?"

"Yes, exactly."

"What about soda pop as compared to orange juice?"

"The soda pop has been carbonated, and the sugar is refined. The caffeine is a stimulant, so what you get is a vehicle that drives too fast and pops wheelies in the middle of the work day, and all its natural sweetness has turned to sugarcoated lies."

"Sugarcoated lies?"

"Yes, the lie is just the truth manipulated into a form that will eventually implode," the voice explained. "Self-gratification is like that; it always implodes."

"And the orange juice?"

"If the orange is grown naturally, then, depending on the way it was handled, juice will be the outcome of the food that is produced. If picked green and dyed orange, it is like a woman or man with dyed hair; you can never tell its true age!"

"What about saints that retain their youthfulness?" asked the woman.

"That is a completely different matter. They use what is known as *siddhis* (spiritual powers). If siddhis are used for self-gratification, they too will implode."

"The person would not be much of a saint if they did that!" said the woman with brown hair far beyond the age common for losing one's hair color.

"The truth of all matter is in the intent. If we are trying to uplift the consciousness of mankind, we are doing a service. If we are glorifying the body for no other reason but to ensure our popularity by gaining wealth and fame, then the results will implode. Think back to your own circumstances."

"Mine?" asked the lady.

"Yes. Remember when you were a teenager?"

"Yes, I dyed my hair blonde. The dark roots kept coming faster and faster. I didn't like that at all. Much of my time was spent examining my hair and trying to figure out how to keep the secret of the hair dye."

"Yes. And then what happened?"

"I went swimming one day, and the chlorine turned it green."

"Exactly! And then?"

"I dyed it black to cover the green, and it turned to straw!"

"Well, I think that explains clearly the need for keeping your focus on dharma instead of self-inflicted pains."

"But I do not want to write to my teacher. I'm shy!"

"Well, he's waiting," said the voice. "Do it now, or do it later."

"Oh! I hate these tests!"

"The Truth will set you free," said the voice, and the telephone began to ring.

"Hello?" said the woman.

Nothing.

That's strange, she thought, but as she went to hang up the receiver, a very clear thought came to her.

I love you, came the thought, with no distinction of race, color, caste, creed, intelligence, or gender.

Once again, she started to put the phone down, and then she wondered, *Could it be my teacher? No!*

The phone remained quiet.

"Master, if this is you, I love you very much. I always wanted to be part of the group closest to you but didn't know how. You let Sita carry the candy, Bhavani brought your chalkboard, Ma cared for you, Anuradha helped run another yoga center, and everyone seemed to be closer to you than me. You asked about their families, and when they were sick you even went to see them in the hospital, but nothing I ever did seemed to win your favor."

Click. The phone hung up.

That is too creepy! thought the woman, but somehow she felt better.

The impending doom that had seemed to float above her was now gone, and the air felt crystal clear. She needed to lie down for a few minutes. Her knees felt kind of weak, and she didn't understand what had just happened.

"When the windshield of the car is dirty, you may cross over the line," the voice had said. "If another car is coming from the opposite direction, you may be killed or, worse, kill someone or something through your neglect to clean the windshield."

I wonder if telling the truth to the proper source is the way to clean the windshield, she thought, lying down on the living room floor.

Her temples began to throb as time and space lifted into a realm different from her normal consciousness. *What's going on?* she thought, but slowly her thoughts fell away. As she was transmuted into light, nothing was left except one bright star far up in the sky.

When the man came home, he was confused by the disappearance of the woman he still called wife. He looked in every corner of the house, but she was nowhere to be found.

She likes to meditate, he thought, but something pulled him toward the window.

My, it's bright out today! Where could my wife be?

"My husband," a glimmering voice said behind him. "You do not understand yet, but one day you will. Clear your mind of selfishness, and keep your focus on the divine. Then and only then will we be one."

The man did not understand. *Where is my wife?*

"I am right here," said the woman. "The truest form of trust comes in revealing your inner heart. The more honest we can get, no matter what the procedure, the more simply we can shine."

The husband had always wanted to tell the truth, but he was afraid.

"What if people laugh?" he asked, thinking his wife feared nothing.

"Oh, that's not true," came her voice again.

"I need to see you!" he demanded. "I'm not going to talk to the empty air like I'm crazy."

Suddenly, one of the lights in the sky moved through the atmosphere. Like a shooting star, it hurled through space, and his wife materialized right before his eyes.

"It's you!" he cried. "Please stay with me until I can attain the state you're in. I'm so afraid to walk alone, and I miss seeing you when you're not here."

"Okay," said the woman. "But for no reason can you reveal my true identity to anyone. If people think a being is fully realized, they become afraid to approach them."

"Are you fully realized?" asked the man.

"Yes, but my cover will prevent you from knowing it from this day forward. Just remember one thing—nothing else matters."

"What?" he asked, almost in tears.

"The tears you cry are the rivers of dharma springing forth from the purity of your heart. The fountain of youth is just that—impossible to be found in a bottle, on some shelf in a pharmacy, or in a drug dealer's home."

"Why are you shining like that?" he asked.

"Because God's glory can't be dimmed. We can tune into it or shut it out; it's our choice. I've chosen to tune into it, and I advise you to do the same."

The man got down on both knees. He had done it before many years earlier, only then it was on a single knee. He'd asked the woman to marry him, even without a ring.

"That won't happen again!" he said. "The next time I ask you to marry me, I'll have a diamond this big!" He held up his fingers to demonstrate the size.

"Don't think about rings anymore," said the woman. "Think only of peace, and everything else will happen on its own."

"Peace?" asked the man. "We used to say that a long time ago, remember?"

"No, we used to repeat the hippie saying that was popular at the time—'peace, love, dope.' We had no idea what we were saying and just got involved with whatever was fun, without thinking of the consequences of our actions."

The woman's light was returning to its normal frequency, and the man had already forgotten what he'd seen a few minutes before.

"Hon'?" he said, like she spoke to her daughter.

"Yes, dear?" she said, responding with every bit of kindness that was who she truly was.

"You are going to leave one day and go to an ashram, aren't you?" He laughed, and then he became very serious. "Are you?"

"Yes," she said in all earnestness. "But the only reason I will go is to take you along with me. I want to show you the marvelous temple my teacher built a long time ago."

"He built it?" asked the man.

"Yes, he built it with a lot of help from his students on the spiritual path."

"Were you one of those who helped?" he asked, and she gave him a hug.

"That's not so important anymore," she said. "Let's go outside and see what the kids are doing."

When they went outside, everything looked different. Off in one corner of the yard was a tree that the man passed every day on his way out of the driveway.

"I never even saw that tree before," said the man.

"I know," said the woman. "It's a nice tree, don't you think?"

"Yeah," he said, blinking a few times. "The sun is really bright today!"

"Yes, it is," agreed the woman.

"And I feel all warm inside, almost as though the sun is reaching into my heart."

"Great," said the lady.

"No, I don't think you understand," he said. "The rays of the sun seem to be penetrating deep into my soul."

"Really?" she responded quietly.

"Yes," he answered with a simple smile.

Just then the neighbor's little boy came over.

"Hey, mister, you look really happy, and there is light shining all around you."

"You know why?" asked the man.

"Why?" replied the little boy.

"Because I am so happy to see you!"

And the man chased the little boy around and around the yard until they both fell down laughing.

And the woman was very glad.